Fredk: Wolsey

ENGLISH FAIRS

ENGLISH FAIRS

IAN STARSMORE

T & H

THAMES AND HUDSON · LONDON

STUDIES IN
INDUSTRIAL ARCHAEOLOGY

GENERAL EDITOR: *Richard Storey*

1 (Frontispiece) Hand-painted rounding boards on a fair-ground stall

Filmset and printed in Great Britain by
BAS Printers Limited, Wallop, Hampshire

CONTENTS

FOREWORD

Fairs are at one and the same time familiar places of amusement and uncanny worlds encompassing a multitude of hidden mysteries and possessing all the fascination of the unknown. The questions people ask about these travelling machines and shows are never-ending; they stem from the insatiable curiosity that fairs arouse in young and old alike. How old are fairs? What sort of people are the showmen? Who builds the rides and roundabouts? Aren't fairs dying out? The chapters of this book, based as they are on the two major components of fairs, festival and its expression in nomadic structures, follow the sequence of these questions. The first chapter examines the historical origins and characteristics of fairs; chapter 2 looks at a present-day fair and shows how it operates, from arrival to departure; chapter 3 covers the technical history of the rides from 1870 to the 1950s, a decade when many modern designs were introduced; chapter 4 discusses fairground equipment, now made in many parts of the world, and takes a look into the future; the final chapter is an exploration of the essential nature of the travelling fair, in which an attempt is made to discover what part it plays in society.

The field of study is large, and much has had to be omitted owing to lack of space, but the main purpose of the book is to illustrate the kind of inventive ability required of all those concerned with the fairground business, particularly the showmen. The energy and skill shown by the best of them are remarkable and seldom given the recognition they deserve.

Imagine for a moment that you have to dismantle an architectural structure measuring some 40 ft by 60 ft, and 30 ft high, by 4 o'clock tomorrow morning, and then transport it, your home and family to a town which may be anywhere from 30 to 200 miles distant. This will give you some idea of the large and complex problems that have been encountered and resolved by showmen almost every week for the past 100 years. Their solutions are practical, enchanting and quite unique.

It must be borne in mind that a photograph taken of a piece of fairground equipment currently in use may well be out of date a few months later, because the designs are changing with such rapidity; nevertheless the details remain true for their time, and – more important – in principle.

Most of us have felt the 'pied piper' effect of the fair and the magnetism exercised by the large covered vehicles, the rides and shows. What has been attempted here is to follow the evolution and development of a variety of fairground devices, to examine each one in detail; for when we visit a fair we tend to be dazzled by its outward trappings, and it has often moved on before we have had time to look beneath the surface.

In mentioning those who have helped in the preparation of the book, I am reminded of a remark once made by Groucho Marx, to the effect that he wouldn't consider joining any club which would have him as a member. It must sometimes be a dubious honour to be thanked for help in the writing of a book, and I might have to ask for the usual forgiveness not only of those omitted from the names listed below, but also of those included in it, were it not for the fact that I know them all to be very nice people with a generous sense of humour, who have also shown a lot of faith in the ideas expressed in this book. Richard Storey and the editorial staff of Thames & Hudson have shown much patience in its preparation, and a great deal of any credit must go to them for their positive and precise criticism. Vic Walker, a truly marvellous craftsman who worked for many years at Savage Ltd, King's Lynn, has supplied priceless and invaluable information. My thanks must go to all the showmen of my acquaintance, including J. R. Bugg, J. C. Bugg, C. Thurston, F. Sedgwick, C. W. Abbott, and H. Botton Jr, as well as to my friends in the Faculty of Art and Design, Leeds Polytechnic, who have given much in the way of ideas and encouragement. There are many others whom I ought to mention for their praise or astonished suspicion, but space does not allow – which may be just as well, since to make distinctions and draw conclusions would be invidious.

1 ORIGINS AND CHARACTERISTICS

This facility with which children satisfy their imagination is a token of the spirituality of their artistic concepts. The toy is the child's initiation into art, or rather, it is his initiation into its practical application, and when he has come to man's estate no perfect work of art will ever arouse in him the same warmth, or the same enthusiasm, or the same confidence.

Charles Baudelaire, *Le monde littéraire* 1853

'*Play is older than culture*' Johan Huizinga

2 Bartholomew Fair: wheel device of 1728 (after H. Morley)

In Britain every year more than 7,000 fairs are held, each of which is, by some strange alchemy, both a mechanical apparition and an Aladdin's Cave of candy-floss, glitter, noise and illusion. On the surface fairs are familiar to us all, whether we go as regular patrons, occasionally taking the children for a treat, or on impulse; yet little is generally known about how they work or the lives of those who run them. They are after all like foreign places which disconcertingly come to us, complexes of exotic architecture peopled by showmen about whom we know next to nothing and whom we therefore suspect of all kinds of hocus.

We all know well the awesome speed of the machines tempting us to experience the dubious pleasures of vertigo and gyrations that literally take the breath away. The faces of the riders, showing a range of emotion from laughter to a horror which increases with the acceleration of the machines, are lost in a blur of speed as they are carried away yelling or giggling in their brilliantly painted cars among the illuminations. The spectacle can be astonishing to watch, as people of all types, ages and sizes are whirled through space, sometimes upside down, at perilous speeds. It is surprising to note, however, that the most voluble of screamers often volunteer to undergo the same ordeal several times in an evening with apparent eagerness. For the more sedate there are the old-time Gallopers, which proceed at a more or less human pace giving everyone a chance to see and wave to their favourite relative on terra firma. The music from the organs which accompany the Gallopers attracts enthusiasts who stand for hours or days in light and dark, sun and snow, with tape recorders attached to their chests, apparently hypnotized by the grandeur and glamour of the unique sounds of clashing cymbals and abruptly braying trumpets, or the serious and sudden movements of the tiny wooden figures, and the splendid arrogance of the shining steeds. How many winter evenings will be spent thumbing through photographs, listening nostalgically to the recordings of old tunes, and telling tall stories of the various rides! The Galloper is a machine to be reckoned with – one which can cast a potent spell.

Another kind of thrill is provided by the Dodgems, onto which everyone can venture, squashing into the tiny cars, feet clicking the floor pedals in anticipation of the commencement of the ride, and then off, in a swerving, dodging parody of motorway lanesmanship. Once in these cars, who knows who owns the Rolls and who the Mini? Sparks fly from the wire ceiling and the wheels trundle round over the aluminium surface of the 'road' and the diminutive colourful cars gain a true hold over the imagination of their occupants, as they bump and dodge their way around the track in veritable 'transports of delight'.

The ubiquitous coconut shies never fail to attract, and the crowds hover around the darts stall, considering seriously the size and weight of the darts, the value of the prizes and chance of success or failure, as caution and suspicion battle with the irresistible urge to gamble and have a go. The inexpensive and fragile pottery figures or glass vases, and the oddly pink monkeys assume a magical guise in the fantasia of a genuine and intoxicating artificiality. This is a theatre of extremes, a brash and absurd mixture of palpable illusions. The whole affair is an artificial landscape, made without thought for what is comme il faut; in

3, 4 Sedgwick's Menagerie, *c.* 1890. All set up (3); on the road (4)

which there are creations of all colours and kinds relating to many aspirations and fears. It adds up to a synthetic adventure in unnatural movements and sounds, and yet it defaces nature very little, leaving as it does only the few wheel tracks on the ground which are washed away with the rain or overgrown with new grass.

The fair is fundamentally 'against nature', expressing a desire to imitate, falsify, construct and distort for our own pleasure, but despite its brashness it is also permanently transient, disappearing as quickly as it came. Who hasn't stood in a fair surveying the enormity of the structures and suddenly wondered where on earth they came from, or conversely what becomes of them when the show is over? This strange and yet familiar scene can vanish until next year, and yet we scarcely realize that it has gone. We may occasionally glimpse a lorry and covered truck or wagon on the road, and eye it curiously, half wondering about its possible destination, and those densely populated and mysterious townships of wagons and caravans which are the homes of the showmen always excite interest. There is undoubtedly something curiously beguiling about a travelling fair, having as it does all the elements of surprise, excitement, mystery and the added ability to vanish over the horizon, away from the familiar to new places, and new sights.

Fairs originate in the desire to entertain and to travel, and the two photographs of Sedgwick's Menagerie illustrate these qualities very graphically. Taken in the 1890s, they

mark the two stages in the transformation of people into performers and empty ground into theatre, which are essential to the mystique of the travelling fair. The metamorphosis of the wagon train into the arena required extraordinary showmanship on the part of the owners, who appear so workmanlike in the picture on the previous page and parade so flamboyantly in the one that faces it.

Historically speaking both economic and religious significance attaches to the fairs, although in time, as we shall see, these two aspects grew increasingly divorced from one another, resulting in the emergence of the fairs we now know. Authors like T. F. G. Dexter or Alfred Watkins have suggested that the real beginnings are to be found in prehistory in the ceremonial games held near barrows, stone circles and boundaries; in Ancient Greece, at such places as Delphi, Corinth and Delos, fairs were associated with the funeral games while in Syria and Rome booths, tents and wooden stands for shows are known to have been used. The Romans themselves may have initiated many fairs in Britain, including the one still held on Newcastle Town Moor. The Saxons and Normans broadened these activities, and since the Norman kings were of the Catholic faith, the fairs were often instituted in the interests of the Church. For many hundreds of years the fairs evolved as vital centres of trade. From the 10th century onwards important trading festivals took place across the Channel at major towns like Bruges and Ghent as well as in England, at such places as Nottingham, Colchester and Norwich. Several fairs were established by Charter under King John, for example at King's Lynn and Stourbridge (near Cambridge), and trade continued to expand. Surprisingly small seaside villages such as Blakeney in Norfolk were then vital ports, filled with foreign vessels busy with the shipment of various produce. Eastern England grew rich through this kind of trade and the greater part of the commerce of this country was carried on at fairs like Stourbridge, which became one of the most important in the world. Stourbridge received its Charter in 1211 and was the main fair in England for hops and wool until 1855 when it closed as a trade mart, although the present-day Cambridge Midsummer fair is its successor. During the Middle Ages, Britain and the countries of Western Europe had trading connections with large fairs in more distant countries like Russia, and it was common for English, Dutch and French merchants to visit Moscow, Kursk, Odessa and other towns where the more important of these took place. It is clear therefore that nomadic trading has a very long tradition which pre-dates the establishment of fixed trading centres by many hundreds of years.

In 1120 Rahere, Henry I's jester, who founded Bartholomew Hospital and Monastery and became the first Prior, received from his king a Charter for the establishment of the fair in London which became known as Bartholomew Fair, and was for many years important as the main cloth fair in England. After the Dissolution the City of London became the 'owners' of the fair, which had grown into a centre for drama of all kinds, mystery plays and puppet shows. Unfortunately, in keeping with the violent character of the age, it was also the scene of religious persecution of all kinds, as were many fairs, including King's Lynn Mart. The last 'Martyr Fair' was in 1611 when the victim was Bartholomew Leggatt, burnt for not recognizing the Athanasian and Nicene Creeds, by order of John King, who was then newly made Bishop of London.

Not until the 17th century did things become more carefree. By this time Bartholomew Fair had begun to present satirical theatre and circus, and almost immediately came in for the heavy criticism and censorship which were the eventual causes of its demise. Attempts were made to suppress stage plays, or puppet shows, in nearly every decade of the fair's existence, notably in 1604, 1647, 1678, 1755 and 1769. In 1691 and 1708 the Authorities attempted to confine the fair to three days instead of 14, complaining that the booths in Smithfield were of 'extraordinary largeness, not occupied by dealers in goods, merchandise, etc., proper for a fair, but used chiefly for stage plays, music. . . ' This may have been so, but Samuel Pepys obviously had not felt as they did when, on the 28th August, 1688, he went twice round Bartholomew Fair, which he was 'glad to see again after two years missing of it by the plague' . . . 'and there did see a ridiculous little stage play called Marry Audrey, a foolish thing, but seen by everybody, and so to Jacob Hall's dancing of the ropes, a thing worth seeing and mightily followed . . .'

In 1728 Henry Fielding, the author of *Tom Jones*, had a booth on the fair, which he kept for about nine years. He put on many plays, most of them no doubt full of innuendo and ribaldry, including *The Beggar's Opera*, which received its first performance in 1728, *Le Médecin Malgré Lui* by Molière, *Love and Jealousy* (*The Downfall of Alexander the Great*), and two plays by an ex-prompter from Drury Lane, *The Generous Free Mason* and *The Emperor of China*. The following quotation from Fielding's own notebooks gives some idea of the qualities which he felt were required of a showman:

> I will, as we say, take you behind the scenes. First then, a valuable actor must sleep in the pit, and wake early to sweep the theatre, and throw fresh sawdust into the boxes; he must shake out the dresses, and wind up and dust the motion jacks; he must teach the dull ones how to act, rout up the idlers from the straw, and redeem those that happen to get into the catch-house. Then sir, when the fair begins, he should sometimes walk about the stage grandly and show his dress; sometimes he should dance with his fellows; sometimes he should sing; sometimes he should blow the trumpet; sometimes he should laugh and joke with the crowd, and

give them a kind of touch-and-go speech, which keeps them merry and makes them come in. Then sir, he should sometimes cover his state robe with a great coat, and go into the crowd, and shout opposite his own booth, like a stranger who is struck with its magnificence: by the way, sir, that is a good trick, I never knew it fail to make an audience; and then he has only to steal away and mount his stage and strum and dance and sing and trumpet, and roar over again.

The fair at its grandest in the 18th century included many attractions 'to gratify the multitude in their wandering and irregular thoughts': Fire-eaters, Theatres, Menageries, Bellringers, Punch and Judy, moving Wax Works, Puppet Shows, Impersonators, Jugglers and Comedians like Lee and Harper who were, by all accounts, a sort of Laurel and Hardy. Harper was the chief comedian, and was large, fat and round-faced 'with a jolly laugh'. A contemporary of theirs was a comedian called simply 'Fawkes' whose name appears in one of Hogarth's prints of Burlington Gate. Although he was the most important professional juggler in the days of George I, we know little about him except that by the time he died on the 25th May, 1731, he had made £10,000 with his shows!

In 1825 Atkins's menagerie boasted an Elephant upwards of 10 feet high and five tons in weight! His consumption of hay, corn, straw, carrots, water, etc. reputedly exceeded 800 lb daily! Eight musicians in scarlet Beefeaters' coats and with skin caps played outside the menagerie, and a stentorian showman drowned the music with his chants of 'Don't be deceived. The only Lion and Tigress in one den that are to be seen in the Fair, or the proprietor will forfeit one thousand guineas. Walk in! Walk in!' A showman by the name of Richardson had a booth lined with green baize, festooned with crimson curtains, and lighted with 1500 variegated lamps. His money-takers sat in elaborate seats, and he had a band of ten performers dressed as Beefeaters, who led a most impressive and dramatic parade. A very fat man called Samwell sporting a tight satin jacket had a troop of tight-rope dancing children and a Dancing Horse. We might well take leave of them and this period with what must have been an often heard introduction to one of the shows, replete with Tumblers, Mechanical Muses and 'Le Ballet de Badinage Champêtre' with a complete band of hautboys, violins, trumpets and kettle-drums:

'All the decorations entirely new. To begin every day at one o'clock, and continue till eleven at night. The fair begins tomorrow at one o'clock!'

One day in 1855, alas, one o'clock came and the fair did not open; it had been forced to close because of mounting pressure from outside. Happily, it has recently re-opened after an interval of over a hundred years. Yet most fairs did manage to survive intact during that period, ready to move into and adapt to the succeeding ages of technology.

5 Bartholomew Fair: Lee & Harper's booth (after H. Morley)

Judith and Holophernes
Lee
Harper
Lee & Harper
is Here
AT
Lee and
Harper
Great Bo

Opposition to fairs in the mid-19th century was of several kinds, partly snobbish, political and puritanical, but also occasioned in part by a fear of disorder. The fairs had often tended to become a riot in more senses than one, particularly as their importance as centres of trade waned; when trade was active, too, there were often disagreements which ended like a scene from a Marx Brothers film. In 1815 for example, at Nottingham, a scuffle took place over the price of cheese. The farmers were asking from 28 to 30 shillings per hundred; this so infuriated people that their violence burst forth like a torrent – cheeses galore were rolled down Wheeler Gate and Peck Lane, and the Mayor in his anxiety to restore peace was knocked down by one.

The main business conducted at Nottingham in the early part of the 19th century was in lace, willow basketry, cheese, poultry and geese, but all this was affected by social changes which took place during Queen Victoria's reign. As transport and communications improved, trading at fairs diminished. Shopkeepers in town had no difficulty in maintaining stocks, and people living in rural areas began to have readier access to the towns by rail; thus there was no longer any need for regular mobile fairs at which people could stock up with supplies. The booths on the fairs, ever since Fielding's time, had presented an opportunity for the satirical treatment of almost anything remotely respected, and this also was a cause for concern among those who were suspicious of the fairs, believing that these, like the theatres, abounded in drolls, comedies, interludes and farces which might 'poison the minds of the populace'.

Another reason for the change from the old-style fairs was that as people became more urbane they began to lose interest in entertainments such as wrestling, skittles or riding the donkey which had once been so absorbing, but which they no longer found sophisticated enough. Therefore, when mechanically-powered rides began to appear at the end of the 19th century, they found ready waiting for them a public which was prepared for something new, and the parting of the ways for the circus and the fair followed shortly on the appearance of the amusement machine. Rides powered by man or horse had been known at fairs as early as the 17th century, and the wheels in the illustrations of Bartholomew Fair are unmechanized versions of the machines of today. Wheels of almost identical form had also appeared in Russia where they were known as *katcheli*; they can still be seen in use in Albania, Siberia and Palestine, and are thought to have derived from wheels used for irrigation purposes; during local festivals children would be given pleasure rides in the water buckets. These primitive swings and roundabouts formed the basis for the evolution of the steam-powered rides which gave the fairs their new lease of life, and transformed them into entertainments to match the industrial revolution.

It was at this time of doubts surrounding the worth of the fairs and when the new type of fair was emerging, that the single most serious attack on the showman's life-style was launched: in 1889 George Smith, M.P. brought in the Movable Dwellings Bill, which, by its emphasis on registration and continuous re-inspection of showmen's homes, would have driven them off the roads. Between 1884 and 1889 Smith had been an active opponent of people with a migratory way of life, beginning with the canal workers. The Liberty and Property Defence League, seeing the dangers inherent in the Bill, wrote to the most prominent showmen of the day, including Joe Caddick the photographer (cf. Ill. 63), whose letters and articles to the press for two years prompted support from many influential people, including Gladstone. The final outcome was that the Bill was defeated, and the showmen, forced to stand together, formed the Van Dwellers' Association, out of which grew the Showman's Guild of Great Britain with its twelve administrative areas covering the whole of the country.

The Bill in a curious way reflects another kind of attack on fairs which can still be observed today, one which is based on an irrational mistrust of the nomadic way of life. Certainly George Smith's attack back-fired somewhat when the doctors and health inspectors he sent to investigate the sanitary conditions of the showmen, reported that they had scarcely seen such a healthy group of people, and incidentally remarked that they themselves would rather like to take a long trip in the beautiful wagons they had seen, which they greatly admired. Travelling peoples have always lived under some suspicion (the most extreme example was in Hitler's Germany), mainly because they are nomadic and are regarded as homeless by those whose idea of home is a building which is a permanent fixture.

The offensives waged on the modern fair have come increasingly in a bureaucratic guise. The fair, like all theatre, relies upon a capacity for rapid adaptation in response to demands which are always changing. As cities grow, land becomes harder to maintain for winter quarters as interested parties press for land to build on; and street fairs are always under pressure from the motor-car. But in spite of this fairs are more popular than ever, and far-seeing councils are giving support to the travelling fairs, not only because they recognize their importance as heritage but also because they are increasingly aware that fairs bring life and colour to town and city centres which are dying as shopping areas and offices force people to live farther and farther out in the suburbs.

The isolation in which showmen live and work owing to being constantly on the move has in many ways given them the strength and craft necessary for survival. Circumstances have always compelled them to be more self-sufficient than those in other walks of life. 'They learn to be handy with the paint-brush, the joiner's tool, they become acquainted by practical experience with steam engines and tractions, four-wheel drives, motor cars, etc., which in many cases they can handle and manipulate with the best . . .' (*The World's Fair*, 1926). The wagons, rides and means of transport have often been made and designed by the itinerant showmen themselves, usually with great skill and expertise. For example, the photograph below shows, in its almost finished state, the wagon which Roy Prestney made for himself and his family; the Shooting Gallery built as part of the lorry was also made by him. This sort of activity has been part of the life of a showman for over a hundred years. Since the beginning of the 19th century wagons have been made in this way, and quite often large manufacturers seem to have begun, quite justifiably, by using the insights which travellers have discovered with their 'system' of practical invention. Showman Raymond Armstrong is reported to have made a marvellous wagon out of a 40 ft container unit. Matthew Taylor and his sons, who belong to the Scottish section of the Guild, have built and decorated two beautiful machines, a 'Dive Bomber' and a trailer-mounted 'Paratrooper' for which they took out patents. Much of the colourful painting is done by showmen like John Bell and Norman Fendick. John says that he designs and paints a single area as one, and that solutions to the visual problems come into his mind al-

6 Roy Prestney's wagon

ready complete, rather than section by section. The shapes and colours themselves seem to be very personal and some showmen attach great importance to them.

The superstructure of the trucks and load-carrying lorries is usually built by the showman/owner, and the way in which ex-Service vehicles are adapted is remarkable (p. 35). Travelling showmen have much to offer society as a whole, especially as they are the main group of people to have remained fully nomadic while using 20th-century technology, and their homes and equipment, as the chapters that follow will show, are some of the very few fully evolved forms of mobile architecture in existence. The structure of the society, with its close family links, but emphasis on independence and imagination, is unique, and is reflected in the way fairs are arranged, rides set up and dismantled. There are endless examples of the way showmen have built or altered their own equipment and only a few can be mentioned in this book, but this type of activity is a vital part of the evolution of the fairground machine. There can be no final or definitive version of fairground history, except in broad terms, because of the enormous number of variations, all of them the expressions of individual inclination.

Nowadays the fairground people come from various backgrounds. Despite long-standing affiliations between gipsy and travelling showman, only a very small percentage are of Romany origin. There are many more whose families have been in the business for the past four or five generations, or whose forebears have been itinerant entertainers for centuries, according to church records. Wherever they come from, their liveliness and resilience is the raison d'être of fairs, and the colour, light and music is an expression of it.

These are some of the general historical and social conditions which have formed the character of the fairground. The vitality of the long tradition of itinerant trading and theatre is still strong in the texture of the modern amusement fairs, expressed in the language of television, film and pop music. Not surprisingly the fairs have survived the threats posed by these potential rivals for our favours, by assuming some of their qualities and imagery. A visit to the fair is still a unique experience, particularly for the children, whose first visit will be remembered with startling clarity just for its sheer physical presence. The collection of marvels persists against all reason in its ability to entice and mystify, and fairgrounds everywhere from Nottingham to Hampstead Heath are full on Saturday nights with people hoping to win a coconut, munching toffee-apples, riding in Dodgems or simply watching the electric machines. But for a while anyway let us break the spell, stop the action and try to find some of the answers to our questions, and travel to a real modern fair to see just how the whole thing works, is put together, where and by whom.

2 THE FAIRGROUND OF TODAY

7 Horses from Noyce's Gallopers at King's Lynn; half-legendary creatures inhabiting a world of fantasy, which may not however be as innocent as first appearances might suggest. Freudians could have a field-day with the elements of competition and submission, and there is more than a hint of Apocalyptic horses in the primitive grimace of the animals as they revolve in repetitive formation. They aren't smiling, they're gnashing and champing, and every line of their carved bodies describes a wildness which is fortunately not expressed in their real speed.

On a more pragmatic note, the irons mentioned in the text can be seen extending from the underside of the horses. With reference to the structural ideas discussed at the end of chapter 5 it is worth noting that the traditional set of Gallopers is held together by its own weight, which tightens the attachment of the swifts to the centre wheel.

The roundabouts and stalls which make up the modern fair do not move from town to town always as a unchanging group; they split up to travel in different directions, and the attractions on a fairground, say in London, may be the same ones which in turn visit places as far apart as Glasgow or Taunton. Showmen who stand next to each other on the final day of a fair may be separated by hundreds of miles on the day following. They often take widely differing routes which may vary slightly from one year to the next and they may meet in a particular grouping only once or twice during that time. This dispersed kind of activity is archetypal in pattern, and has remained essentially the same since the days when horses or steam engines were in common use, so that a study of any single fair will tell us a lot about the many others. Norwich fair, which takes place every Easter and Christmas, is typical and provides an attraction which draws thousands of people from 30 or 40 miles around. The side-shows, stalls and rides to be seen there travel over many parts of Great Britain, and the detailed descriptions of them will give information about the general principles of the assembly of fairs everywhere.

Most outside observers get a wholly misleading impression of chaos when they see a fair newly arrive at a site and begin to set itself up. In order to discover how systematically everything is in fact arranged it is necessary to 'go back to the drawing-board'. The plans for a large fair are usually drawn up by those in charge in close co-operation with the local council, who then leave the mechanics of the layout and assembly to the showmen themselves. The revenue gained from the fairs by the council can be very large, and is payable to them by an agreed amount per footage as shown on the plans; the owner of a large mechanical ride 50 feet in diameter would pay the appropriate price for that size of ride, and the payment for a machine is normally greater per foot than the price charged for stalls.

The showmen apply for ground for their stall or ride to the council or owner of the land on which a fair is to be held, or sometimes to another showman who may be the lessee of the whole area for one or two weeks annually. Advertisements appear regularly in the showmen's newspaper *The World's Fair*, offering space for Dodgems or other much needed entertainments at many fairs throughout the year. Under the regulations of the Showmen's Guild, once

MERRY

a showman has reserved ground he must appear consistently at that fair, and may not sub-let the ground for more than two consecutive years, if he is to retain his right to that space. Most showmen have a regular annual run; this may begin anywhere in the season which lasts from February 14th, with the opening of King's Lynn Mart, to 'back end time' in November when there are many 'mops' and fairs celebrating Guy Fawkes Day. There are also several special fairs for Christmas, of which Norwich is one. The colder months however are usually spent in 'winter quarters', on land owned privately or by the Guild, where for once the wagons become stationary homes, and time can be found to carry out complete repairs of the equipment. There are only a few fairs before Easter-time, so that while some of the showmen who visit Norwich may have already been to other towns, for others this is the first fair of their season. Some of them, who belong to the Eastern Counties Section of the Guild, may have spent the winter in Norwich; others may have come from places as distant as Gloucester, but all those who are to be at a fair arrive at a precisely prearranged time for the 'pull-on' prior to the assembly of the structures. During the week of Norwich fair the same procedure will be followed at fairs in London and other towns throughout Great Britain.

The equipment which is described analytically in this chapter does not exist in a vacuum. It owes its existence largely to the showmen who with their energy and vision create, modify and maintain it. The character of their life has changed little over the past hundred years and its centre is the wagon, which in winter is warmer than a house, and in summer derives space and light from the many landscapes through which it moves. Of all the fairground devices the wagon is the one which offers most security and freedom, and contains most closely within its structure the poetic rationale of the fair. But though wagons answer a primitive need for travel they are far from primitive in construction; they can have the most sophisticated equipment, including efficient kitchens, under-floor heating, bathrooms and showers. As living spaces they are, because they have to be, much more efficient and compact than the contemporary house, and have evolved moreover without there being an architect in sight.

Wagons are usually grouped together away from the façades of the open fair, each giving its neighbours shelter and protection from the wind and rain. The close family life, lived in and around these wagons, is the social basis of fairground existence. Family ties are strong; children live a nomadic life, which can include a week-by-week attendance at different schools, and those of them who so wish seem to find no difficulty in gaining places in further education. Since the way of life is itinerant and the home is mobile, families aren't separated by the necessity of going away to work. Domestic tasks themselves are plentiful and shared; anything that can shine is polished, be it interior wood, glass or metal. There is always water to be fetched in gleaming cans from a tap in some corner of the fairground, or from a neighbouring farm. Each week non-fitted furniture, the television set and the rest must be made secure for the journey, and one of the more serious concerns of the showman's wife is the safety of her china as wagons are bounced up kerbs, and over pavements, to squeeze between gates with inches on either side. Fortunately for domestic peace breakages are rare.

Showmen themselves regard their way of life as unexceptional or even mundane, and certainly the long tradition of fairs has involved a constant repetition and continuity of necessary work. The hours are unusual by conventional standards and mean working at week-ends far into the night and early morning, and work is packed into short periods of extreme intensity, particularly on the last day of a fair. Journeys can begin at 5 or 6 a.m., as the lorries and trucks travel through early mists across empty landscapes, making for distant and sleeping towns. The showman has to adjust to both temporal and social demands, yet he leads a life which has a great sense of tradition and which belongs still to the land and seasons much as farming does. The fair is a technological village of extensive dimensions but human proportions: upon reaching a new town friends not seen since the year before can be greeted, stories swapped, a vital conversation continued and news exchanged. From the first moment, therefore, each fair is a way of life, as much a social gathering as a business enterprise, and this is the secret of the vitality of invention and imagination which finds its expression in the equipment which will now be described and illustrated.

* * *

The Norwich Easter Fair has seven machines and numerous stalls, is large enough to be interesting and small enough to describe in some detail . . . Following the arrival of the lorries, loads and wagons at Norwich, normally at about six in the evening, the first task is the difficult one of positioning the wagons in their proper place and making sure that they are level and secure. The business becomes rather like a huge game of chess, and obvious care has to be taken that the man who must leave first puts his wagon in last. Although these 3-ton wagons are difficult to move, much of this type of work must be done by hand because the confined spaces prevent the use of lorries. Even on level ground this clearly requires concentration, strength and skill; unfortunately East Anglia is not as flat as geographers would have us believe and since Norwich Hill slopes in almost every imaginable direction the job becomes ex-

tremely complex, and sometimes resembles an enormous juggling act as wagons are raised several feet in the air in order to give a true perpendicular. The very unevenness of the ground at Norwich is instructive because it reveals what is in general the most essential point in the setting-up of fairs – that they must be stable and level. It requires the true showman's expertise to get the better of sloping, broken and slippery surfaces, and the creation of a level foundation on which to live and work is one of the principal skills.

Within 24 hours of arrival the large rides are positioned and built up. The structures take between four and six hours to erect, depending upon size and the number of men involved, but completion of all the details takes at least a further day because of the positioning of generators, the laying out and connecting of cables, and final testing of lamps, circuits, power systems as well as the structures themselves. These are as much safety checks as they are working necessities. Each component of a machine must be examined every week during the season, and if a part *is* found to be defective it must immediately be replaced, because the ride could not otherwise be erected and made

8 General view of Norwich Fair, showing all the main rides and making clear the overall plan, in which space is regularly divided and enclosed. From front to back the rides are: C. & K. Gray's Octopus, John Remblance's Skyliner, D. Gray's Dodgems, Price's Paratrooper; above these can be seen the tops of Charles Thurston's Swirl (Skid), and Jets; and beyond these C. & K. Gray's converted Noah's Ark, now a Waltzer. Its flat wooden top was constructed by the owners because it is less susceptible to wind damage than a canvas tilt. The elements can be the showman's enemy; in this photograph a light wind is lifting slightly the edges of the Dodgem tilts—a fierce gale can tear them in minutes. Again, snow and ice can freeze a tilt making it impossible to fold; they also render slopes difficult for the vehicles to negotiate.

The main rides are always built and positioned first, and dismantled last; the dismantling of a joint is a race against the time when the rides close and larger vehicles will need access. The illustration gives a good idea of the close and precise arrangements which necessitate definitive and pre-planned action. The machines form a straight line down the centre of the ground, and are surrounded by the stalls, smaller children's rides and shows which form lanes around the fair. The lorries and wagons are beyond these and form the final perimeter of the 'magic' area.

operational. Their very mobility makes them safer, so that travelling fairgrounds tend to have fewer accidents than permanent ones. There are no full-size travelling roller-coasters in this country, and the terrible accident at the Battersea Fun Fair[1] in 1972 could not have happened if the ride had been one which was dismantled and checked every week as are *all* portable machines.[2]

The focal points of any fairground must be the 'rides', although these depend upon the 'joints' and shows which give them space and help to create the necessary atmosphere. An over-all view of the Norwich Fair appears on the opposite page, and the rides which it offers the public are described below, with accompanying photographs illustrating general points of importance and showing some of the qualities of versatility and prefabrication.

The Dodgems appear at both Easter and Christmas at Norwich. The ride is familiar and will reveal many of the characteristics of fairground machines. Dodgems always seem to be popular, and the interest in them on the part of participants and audience alike doesn't seem to vary regionally as is the case with certain other rides, which may perhaps find favour in the West Country but attract little attention in the North, or vice versa; there are no apparent reasons for these variations and fluctuations of interest. One set of Dodgems is based in Norwich and travels mostly in East Anglia, but the parts have typically mixed origins. It was made originally by Supercar (Coventry) Ltd (pp.85–6), although the wood has been replaced entirely by the firm of Taylor in Wroxham (Norfolk). The ride packs onto two lorries and one truck, which were bought from Shell Mex and subsequently adapted, partly by Savage & Co. (pp. 48–53), and partly by the owner, who fitted the generators. Underneath the truck can be found 'belly boxes' containing wooden slats or 'packing', and these form the basis of all rides. Dodgems, like the Swirl or Waltzer, need a lot of support because a large area is covered by a structure which is mostly a static and supporting enclosure. Rides like the Jets (Ill. 104) or the Octopus (Ill. 74) don't require so much since they are usually trailer-mounted and only the weight-bearing points of the mounting touch the ground; all machines however depend for their stability on packing and levelling. Because of the steep slope of the ground at Norwich, barrels are used to support the rides; the showmen visiting the ground have probably been to the same spot for many years and quickly become acquainted with the particular problems associated with it. The barrels and packing provide the support for the underframe of the floor of the Dodgems, each section of which is numbered and lettered, and will fit only into one place, like a piece in a giant jig-saw puzzle. When this first stage is complete the apparatus is in tension and becomes a very stable and self-contained system. The 'plates' made of a wooden base and

1 Being demolished at the time of writing.

2 There is a safety code prepared with great care for *travelling* fairground equipment by the Showman's Guild, in co-operation with the Institute of Municipal Safety Officers and the Royal Society for the Prevention of Accidents.

9 One of the trucks used for transportation of the Dodgems, here uncovered for the first stage of unloading. The diamond-shaped 'principals' are attached to the sides, and behind them are some of the cars and decorative work. The manner of packing and the sequence of operations when setting up or dismantling this ride remain the same at all times.

alloy surface fit into the skeleton of the floor, and lock the whole structure together. Around the perimeter of the floor are the brackets into which the wooden uprights are placed; aluminium lengths hold these together, and the 'principals' span the top to form the roof structure. The 'nets' which connect the current to the cars are inserted into this upper section, and then the 'tilt' is put on. This is only a brief description of the procedure, and does not include the removal of the cars from the truck and lorry, and the constant moving about that installation entails. It takes four hours of intense activity, and all those involved must always know where they should be, and what the general point and purpose of each operation is. Each piece of equipment has its specific place and the informal appearance conceals the necessary craft, sensitivity and control, without which there would certainly be serious and dangerous disorder. The process becomes yet more difficult in reverse, because dismantling must frequently be done in complete darkness.

Electricity, which provides power for the lamps and

10 The Dodgem track being laid from the plate truck. The first of the heavy plates is lifted from the lorry and slotted into the alloy grid jigsaw.

11 Early stages in building up the Waltzer. Beyond can be seen the stacked cars. The winch intruding into the picture has been used to lower the weighty platform down onto the track. The centre truck with its toothed 'cheese wheel' is to the right; from here to the outer track are a series of arms with wheels at the far end which support the platforms and carry them around the undulating track

machines, is produced at 110 volts DC, by generators which revolve at somewhere around 1100 r.p.m. (This low voltage diminishes the chance of accidents originating from the cables.) When electricity is needed for the ride the drive shaft to the lorry's rear wheels is disconnected and re-connected directly to the generator; the mains are then laid out in as straight a line as possible to the ride. Dynamos are often arranged in this way, or raised on separate trucks, on showmens' tractors, or on the vehicles' superstructure.

So much for the basic equipment: machine, transport, and power. The wagon, in this instance a 28 ft Colchester (pp. 81–4), is smaller than many made by the same firm and is an extremely elegant, well designed vehicle for living in. The equipment as a whole fulfils its purpose very well.

The Dodgems described above travel mostly with the Waltzer (pp. 73, 74) and Octopus (p. 35) and the three machines appear at many small fairs in Norfolk. The Waltzer is characteristic of the early modern rides, and part of the 'building-up' sequence can be followed by studying the photograph and caption above.

12 The Colchester wagon (see Chapter 4) at Long Melford, Suffolk, on the same green as the fair of 1906 (see Ill. 27)

13 The Waltzer, Octopus and Dodgems at Blakeney, Norfolk, built on the same spot as the old fair (see Ill. 26), and many months after their annual Easter venue at Norwich, in a hot and rural summer. Roy Prestney's lorry and shooting gallery, mentioned in Chapter 1, are to the right of the photo, above the Octopus.

Charles Thurston is a Norwich-based showman, whose Swirl and Jets, seen together in Ill. 8, travel different routes during the season. Quite often the Jets will be visiting Coventry, Lakenheath and Sheffield, say, while the Swirl is doing the rounds of Oxford, Nottingham and Bridlington. The Swirl is a particularly spectacular ride: built by the firm of J. R. Lakin (Ill. 72) in about 1948, it is especially remarkable on account of its ornamentation by Hall and Fowle, the well-known London firm of showmen's decorators; the cars are outstanding for their beauty, exemplifying magnificent and quite unique fairground decoration at its best. Even when the machine is stationary the cars have a kinetic appearance, suggesting all the excitement and speed which is 'fairground'.

The Jets were built by Langwheels, and collected in September 1957. The older sort of cars with front and rear seats used to be part of this ride; a change of cars was now made so that passengers could sit side by side. The photograph of the lorries which transport the ride may be compared with Ill. 21 taken at Nottingham in the fifties. Showmen will attempt different methods of packing and transportation to meet changing circumstances; such experiments are, and indeed must be, carried out all the time as new problems present themselves and better solutions are discovered. The vehicles which transport these rides are as much a part of the atmosphere of fairs as the rides themselves.

The Paratrooper is owned by a showman based in Gloucester; Norwich is the first fair of the season for this ride and some of the repainting was done while it was there. This particular machine was made about ten years ago under contract to an American firm in Blackpool, although other Paratroopers are made by Ivan Bennett's (p. 86) and Maxwell's (p. 85). The main column is folded in the middle

14 The Jet lorries. The right-hand vehicle is towing the compressor unit; the other vehicle is pulling the compact centre truck.

15 The converted Scammell tractor with generators: Paratrooper vehicles in transit. The centre pole is on the left-hand lorry, its base towards the camera.

when the ride is travelling, and the whole machine packs onto the lorry and trailer, with two lighting sets on the Scammell showman's tractor. In building up, the central column is levelled first, unfolded, and then the arms and finally the cars are attached. The Scammell was purchased from Shell Mex and converted to a tractor providing power for the ride; the two generators are powered by Gardner engines, and the sets were put together by the owner. The tractor, which is similar to the one owned by C. Farrell (p. 39), was operational for the first time at Norwich and was a great success. This Paratrooper travels extensively and forms a part of many fairs: from Gloucester it moves to Norwich, Boston, Wiggin (Lancs.), Runcorn (Cheshire), Ratcliffe (Manchester), Bradford, Keighley, Warrington, Ormskirk, St Helens, Salford, Fleetwood; thence to Hampton Court, Devizes, Oxford, Barnstaple, Bridgwater, Nottingham, Stratford-on-Avon, Banbury, Salisbury, Worcester, Birmingham, and finally back to Gloucester in November.

The Skyliner is an American-designed ride, named 'Rok-o-Plane' in the USA (Ill. 97); it was made by the Eyerley Manufacturing Co., Salem, Oregon, and is a popular machine providing plenty of thrills – a big wheel with freely revolving cars. It is trailer-mounted with four arms permanently attached in a way which is typically American, and more recent rides of this sort have all eight arms as fixtures. These arms are extended or fitted whilst the central column is in a lowered position, then the whole thing is raised hydraulically, and the cars are secured; transport is provided by one eight-wheeled lorry and an

16 The Skyliner packed and in transit. The articulated unit can be detached and used as a base from which the centre pole is raised.

articulated trailer. The machine has been travelling for only five years; previously it was owned by Billy Butlin, who imported the ride into England. It now visits most of the main fairs in the country, including Norwich, Yarmouth, Doncaster, Newcastle, Nottingham, Hull and Durham.

These seven machines are the usual and central attractions of the fair at Norwich but equally interesting are the shows. They are certainly among the most widely travelled of their kind, since any mobile live entertainment must have an extensive route or a frequent change of programme to attract audiences; and if they want to keep in business the owners must show great versatility and ingenuity, must have something of the actor, the musician and the painter in their make-up. From very crude entertainment like this fairs have drawn their energy for centuries; the shows run by the Appleton family obviously have their source deep in human curiosity, and are a link with the early travelling theatres (see p. 13) which have vanished from the fairground scene. On the final day of the Norwich fair the Helter-Skelter, owned by the same family, can be seen packed up ready for its next journey to Wales, while the shows go to Yarmouth. This gives an idea of the great distances covered by these attractions. Based in King's Lynn, they visit places as far afield as Yarmouth, Boston, London, Wembley, Epsom (for the Derby), Stroud (Gloucestershire), Torquay, Brixham (Devon), Babbacombe, Redroof (London again); then they double back to Devizes, Oxford, Hotney

St Mary's (Devon), Bridgwater, Peterborough, Stafford, Banbury, Glastonbury, Menai Bridge (Isle of Anglesey, Wales), Babington (Devon), Titchfield (Hampshire) and Portland (Dorset). These are only some of the towns and villages visited before they return to Lynn in mid-November for the winter. The stops between Menai Bridge and Portland are all one- or two-day fairs, and this family travels continuously for a week, covering well over 1,000 miles. Though the first part of the journey from Menai Bridge to Babington is done overnight, the destination is not reached until 4 o'clock in the afternoon. The shows must then be built and ready to open at 10.00 a.m. the following day, so it is easy to see why energy and initiative are paramount virtues. The equipment is always in first-class condition. The Helter-Skelter travels on two lorries, the other vehicle carries the side shows and a small juvenile roundabout (also built by the owners).

The 'joints' and 'hoop-las' are the colourful and decorative fabric of the fair, containing games which go back through centuries – quoits, skittles, darts, ball games. Only the simpler old-fashioned games seem to survive, and many a newly invented game has been seen to be of little or

17 One of the shows run by the Appleton family

18 The centre truck of Perry Day's Octopus

no interest to the public. Though stalls and shows existed for many hundreds of years without a ride, as we have seen, the machines without the 'joints' wouldn't be a sufficient attraction (p. 24). The 'side-stuff' is mostly all home-made, although some of the round 'hoop-las' are manufactured by professional firms like Knobbs or Barkers. The contents of these stalls, the adornments of ceramics, glass and toys which catch the eye with their allure can seem like treasure to the lucky winners. Nor has this always turned out to be an illusion, for many of the ceramic figures common in 19th-century fairs as prizes are now valued pieces in private collections and museums.

For three or four days of the week the fair is open and we see the spectacle which most of us recognize. Then at about 8 o'clock on the final evening of Norwich Fair most of the 'joints', hoop-las and shows are dismantled. The main rides stay open until about two hours before midnight, and then the disappearing act begins: at 10 p.m. all is light, movement and music, but by 2 a.m. everything is in darkness and the rides have vanished into the night. During these four hours the generators are shut down, electric light bulbs taken out and structures dismantled often in weather which is far from conducive to such uncongenial tasks. The greatest skills are needed in timing the movement of trucks and caravans. The scene changes abruptly from one of bright lights, crowds and chatter to one of darkness through which figures hurry in the increasing cold, balancing heavy and awkward weights on their shoulders, or winding electric cable at a furious rate with numb hands. The architecture which so thrilled the visitors to the fair is robbed of colour by the gloom and becomes barely recognizable as it is dismembered and transformed into piles of painted wood and metal plate. The fairground is soon an empty stage and the transition from an open-air theatre back to a car park is a rapid and brutal process. The final day of a fair is greeted by showmen with mixed feelings. As a rule it is in many ways the most important day for business, but it is also the most tiring. The twelve or fourteen hours of trade must always be followed by these four hours of arduous and difficult work. Nevertheless, next morning most of the showmen are up again at about 6 o'clock—to 'pull away' from Norwich. By the time the first of the city's inhabitants are going to work, most of the loads bound for Yarmouth Fair are well on their way, if not already there.

The equipment we have seen at Norwich characterizes the modern fairground, but much of it has a curious history. The following is a typical example. The photograph on the opposite page shows the centre truck of Perry Day's Octopus, at Long Melford, Suffolk. The truck itself was adapted from an ex-army searchlight carrier, and the powerful Gardner engine which now drives the ride, used to provide power for the searchlight. In this way the designer of the searchlight carrier unwittingly altered the design of an important piece of fairground equipment, since the construction of the truck became the accepted pattern for later rides. Army vehicles served the showman's purpose admirably, particularly as the current used was 110 volts DC. This accounts in part for the extensive use of the 'Matador' and the 'Diamond T', as showman's tractors in the 1950s; these lorries were extremely powerful and could pull three or four loaded trucks with ease. Then the laws governing trailers and lorries were changed and the number of loads which could be towed was limited, with the consequence that these ex-Army vehicles are becoming more scarce on fairgrounds, and eight-wheeled lorries, with a single truck, are taking their place. Perry Day, for similar reasons, intends to dismantle the centre truck and transport the whole load on an extended lorry, as many showmen have done, thus managing with one journey where perhaps three would previously have been necessary. Some examples of the kind of adaptation of equipment that has been effected at different stages of the development of the modern fairground can be seen in the sequence of illustrations that follows.

19 Wagon converted into a freight truck

20 Generator carried by a modern lorry

21 Thurston's 'Diamond T', at Nottingham in the 1950s

22 Sedgwick's electric Tilling Stevens

King's Lynn Mart, where the first fair of the season takes place, has an extremely long history, pre-dating the charter granted by King John. As a fair it presents the visiting showmen with quite different problems from those he encounters at Norwich, but it possesses certain advantages too. The area is a small even shape, and – most important – is quite flat. The problems are therefore more the abstract ones of organization than the sort of physical difficulties experienced on Norwich Hill. The number of machines can be seen from the plan, but two rides in particular from the 1973 fair are interesting because they each belong to a different age. The wheel formation is the basis of most rides, and the Big Wheel itself is not a new machine. There were examples at the 1894 Earl's Court Exhibition in London and at the 1893 Exhibition in Chicago, but the Big Wheel to be seen travelling these days is light, highly mobile and very much part of the 20th century. It remains a very attractive ride built now in large numbers and types by several firms including the 'Big Eli Co.', U.S.A. (see Chapter 4, pp. 90, 92) who made the example shown opposite. On leaving America the ride was bought by the owners of an amusement park, who then sold it to showman Charles Farrell; he says it looked rather bare until he had it decorated by Hall and Fowle. The machine now goes far afield in England, Scotland and Wales, and in the course of the year visits King's Lynn, Hampstead Heath (Easter), Derby,

23 Lay-out of King's Lynn Mart

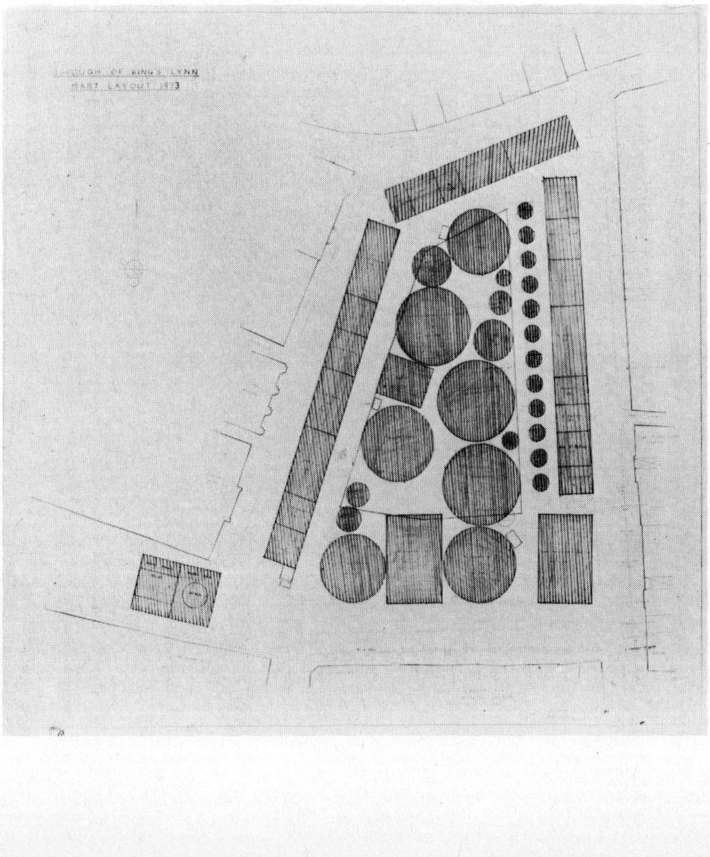

24 Charles Farrell's Big Wheel

Chesterfield, London area (until Whitsun), Cambridge (Midsummer Fair), Glasgow, Northampton, Birmingham area, Hampstead Heath (September Bank holiday), Devizes, Neath (Wales), Northampton, Rushden (Feast), Burton-on-Trent, Baldock, Peterborough, Bedford, Belper (Derbyshire), Loughborough, returning to the Norwich base in November. The most remarkable part of the round journey is that from Cambridge Midsummer Fair to Glasgow, and back to Northampton. A Scammell tractor was purchased from British Oxygen in 1969, and several alterations were done by an engineer in Sheffield (S. Ward), to Mr Farrell's own specifications. The vehicle was lengthened to accommodate the winch at the rear, which is an invaluable device for coping with muddy conditions; a 250 gallon tank was also included to provide fuel for the 'lighting sets'. All the lorries and trucks of this ride are decorated in maroon and gold.

In the process of assembling the Wheel the base is levelled, and the central tower erected, before the spokes are put in one at a time. Props support the first three arms, after which pulleys are used. The tension wires follow, then the Wheel is 'walked round' while the lights are put in. Finally the wire drive is connected.

The most surprising object to be seen at Lynn Mart in 1973 was the set of horses or Gallopers, owned by Jim Noyce & Sons, who are based at Farnborough, Hants. The machine itself is immaculate, and appears at first sight to be new. This is a tribute to the amount of work done by the owners, for although this was only its second visit to Lynn, the first was back in 1885 when it came direct from Savages, the manufacturers (pp. 48–9). It appeared, in all its splendour on a space which Frederick Savage reserved each year for his newest machine. Since then four or five generations of children have ridden on these golden horses. The 19th century produced many strange mixtures of architecture, not all of them beautiful, and it may be that this machine expresses all that was best. It was an extravagant and flamboyant toy, a steam-powered dream, containing architecture, sculpture and painting in a single fantastic circle. The ride was originally commissioned and in part designed by one of the Studt Brothers, but it was eventually bought, in the year of its manufacture, by John Cole, who at that time travelled mainly in the Bristol area, and the machine has remained in the West of England for most of the time since then. There have been many modifications, not the least of which conceals the fact that it is no longer driven by steam. The present owner bought the ride about twenty years ago, when its condition had deteriorated, and he proceeded to restore it, rebuilding many parts. All the work, including carving and painting, has been done by the owners; initially by Joseph Matthews, and Jim Noyce who is now assisted by his sons. The massive centre truck was completely rebuilt, and all the wood replaced with iron in the winter of 1972; twin wheels were put on, and the whole centre lengthened. The 'quarterings' and 'swifts' are also recent renewals. Many of the gold areas of paint are in fact real gold leaf, which is much more lasting than substitutes. Such is the care with which this ride is tended that the whole process of restoration is continuous – no sooner is one thing completed than another is begun. The ride itself has good proportions, and the space is well used. It is the largest of the three-abreast versions made by Savage and Co., and although Charles Manning has a set of four-abreast Gallopers the width – 42 feet – is the same for both. Each machine made by Savages differed in some respect from the others, and this is nowhere better demonstrated than in Gallopers, which could be tall, short, broad, squat, etc. depending on the specifications submitted by the showmen. The Savage-made horses were replaced many years ago by

25 Centre truck of Noyce's Gallopers being pulled up on the gantry, at St Giles Fair, Oxford

the present ones which were individually carved and painted by a Bristol firm called Anderson, who have, unfortunately, long since closed down.

The assembly of this ride in some ways presents more difficulties than newer rides, partly because it is so heavy. The process is a systematic one, and the stages can be numbered in such a way as to approximate to the actual operations. In a simplified form these are:

1 The 'gantry', the base on which the centre truck stands, is levelled.

2 The centre truck is pulled up by wires on 'run-ups' (slopes) onto the gantry.

3 The top pole is fixed in the upright position.

4 The swifts and quarterings are put in place, and are followed by:

5 The rounding boards

6 The tilt (top canvas covering)

7 The bottom organ and bottom centres

8 The platform rods

9 The horse rods

10 The platform quarterings

11 The platforms

12 The steps and horses

The rods which are fastened to the underside of the horses, referred to by fairground people as 'belly irons', were

26 Blakeney Fair at the turn of the century. In the foreground is an old type of Shooting Gallery with a long lead tube through which the gun would be aimed at the target.

originally in one continuous piece. The irons on this machine, however, are in two pieces which bolt together from below, enabling the platforms to be connected first before fixing on the lower section of the rods. The job of putting on platforms used to be more difficult, for the showman had to bend down whilst carrying their enormous weight in order to pass the continuous rods through the platform guides. These guides were the object of much inventive activity in the 1880s, more than might be imagined, their purpose being to control the outward swinging movements of the horses when the ride is in motion.

A feature of this ride is the machine's revolving hub known as the 'cheese wheel', which Frederick Savage invented. This allows the considerable weight of the top and platform to be transferred to the main drive, and at the same time makes possible the up-and-down motion of the horses, via the universal joints and cranks. How it works is shown in Ill. 33 (p. 51).

This is one of the most exceptional machines travelling widely today. Not so many years ago Gallopers changed hands for very little money indeed, but now they have a rarity value and have become almost legendary – the remaining links with the early part of the story of mechanical fairs told in the next chapter. The steam fairs of the late 19th and early 20th centuries, when horses much like these

27 A glimpse into the past. Long Melford Fair, 1906. This fair used to play a very important role in horse trading. The top tilt is off the large machine in the background. One of the showmen appears to be making preparations for departure. The Romany wagons are lined up on the far side. The Shooting Gallery has on its roof a large water tank, providing water pressure to keep the targets moving. The canvases hanging on the sides of the wagons were to prevent the paintwork from damage by sunlight.

were still being used for many of the rides, presented a remarkable spectacle.

In 1922, with the first appearance of the Chairs, a contemporary newspaper published the following description of the scene:

All through the Saturday morning huge crowds of people thronged through the streets, until by midday it was difficult to pass in places. The first to get off the mark on Saturday were the horses opposite the post office. These pigmy equestrians (sic) were careering round well before midday carrying equally diminutive riders. These latter sat their rigid charges with an assurance and palpable pride that was most exhilarating. But the Lilliputian charges outside the post office soon had a host of rivals. On the market place that mysterious collection of chairs and iron chains which had so exercised the minds of those who had watched them being erected now began to give an indication of the purpose to which they were to be put.

'I wouldn't go up in them things for a pension,' said one woman as soon as she saw them started. 'Nor me,' said another with a shudder, 'Not if I know it.' As it happened however these flying swings proved one of the best attractions of the day . . . The faster the thing went round the greater the tilt outwards of the riders and they flew through space with the easy abandon of gulls gliding over a river.

The accompanying old photographs (Ills. 26–28), showing some of these early fairs, will serve to introduce their fascinating history.

28 St Giles Fair, Oxford, 1895. This photograph vividly conveys the happy, care-free atmosphere of the fairground on a sunny day.

3 A TECHNICAL HISTORY

Certainly the part played by toys and non-utilitarian instruments in fostering important inventions cannot lightly be ignored. The first 'use' of the steam engine as suggested by Hero, was to create magical effects in the temple to awe the populace.

Lewis Mumford, *Technics and Civilization* 1931

29 William Reynolds and Charles King, 1885. Rides were built with these double cranks, and appeared at Lynn Mart in February 1886, but they proved clumsy, and more difficult to maintain than the machines with single cranks. Note that there is no platform with this ride, which represents therefore a kind of intermediate stage in the evolution from the 'Dobbies' to the full top-motion Galloper.

The remote horizons and rich farming land of Norfolk provided the background for the introduction of mechanical fairs to Great Britain. Some of the most important names among manufacturers were born and worked there, including Frederick Savage, Robert Tidman, and Charles Burrell. In many significant ways, the whole context was appropriate. The beginning of the second half of the 19th century saw a gradual increase in the use of steam power on farms, and although horses continued in use for a long time, the steam engine was working in combination with ploughs by 1853. Charles Burrell, at Thetford, was in business making portable engines, which were mounted on trucks pulled by horses, for agricultural purposes. In 1862 Thomas Aveling developed the first traction engine for haulage, but although many other similar engines appeared on the scene around the same date, they were little used because of the heavy tolls levied on road vehicles. Therefore the evolution of the basic steam engine, and the type and character of the engineering, took place within the farming communities for whom Savage, Tidman, and Burrell worked. It is a short step in design terms, from the machine in an early Savage catalogue to the kind of mechanics for which Savage was to become famous throughout the world. During the course of his life – he was born in 1828 and died in 1897 – he was responsible for many of the truly important inventions in the history of fairs. His training as an engineer, brazier and tinsmith, his experience with farming equipment, and his acquaintanceship with rural crafts generally gave him all the necessary skills. Natural inventiveness and curiosity did the rest.

Pony-driven rides existed in the early 1860s and one of the first steam rides was seen at Aylsham fair in one of the summers late in the same decade. Savage, who was born near Aylsham, almost certainly saw it there, and very soon

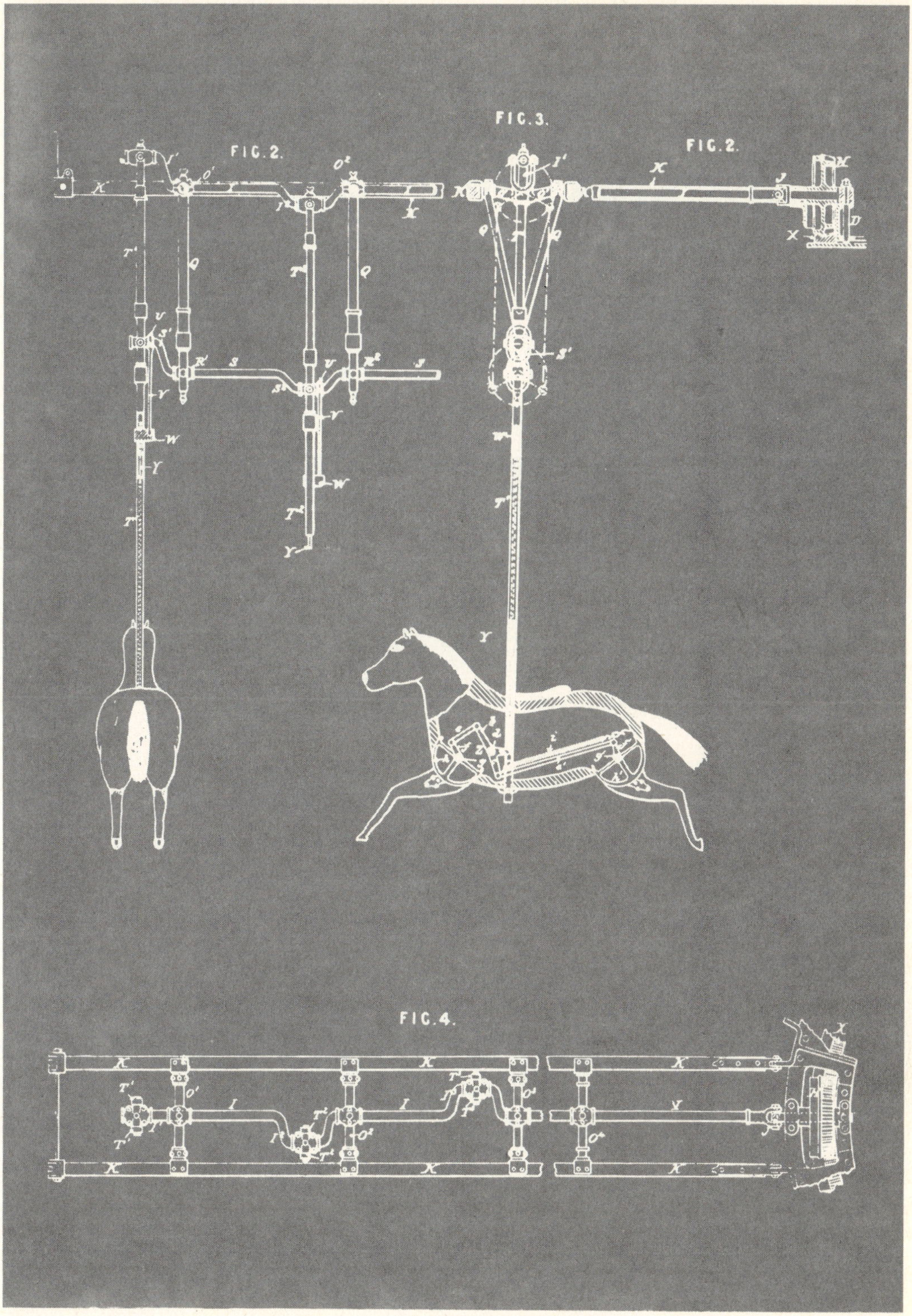
FIG. 2.
FIG. 3.
FIG. 2.
FIG. 4.

afterwards began his career as a manufacturer of steam rides. By all accounts the first of these to be built were the Velocipedes (see p. 99), which followed the invention of the pedal bicycle in France in the 1860s. There has been considerable dispute as to who exactly was the inventor; what is clear, however, is that by 1870 Savage was making steam-powered Velocipedes. In this chapter are illustrated the kinds of machines that were the ultimate expression of inventive fantasy of the period from 1870 to the 1920s. Behind the opulent façades were sound mechanical designs, and it would be useful to glance at some of the puzzles and answers which preoccupied the engineers of the times and see what solutions they offered.

Savages' as a firm were best known for the sets of galloping horses, and the set described in the previous chapter represents the highest pitch of achievement reached. The

30 A Savage engine attached to a ploughing system

earliest 'horses' were simple wooden figures suspended from a revolving top, which was hand-driven, with straight down-pointing legs, rather lifeless in appearance, and were called 'Dobbies'. Both 'top-motion Gallopers' and 'platform Gallopers' were eventually made in large numbers although the former are more widely known. The movement of the horses on the platform version was provided by a system of levers and gears attached to the large wheel underneath each segment of the platform. How the problem of movement in a 'top-motion' set of horses was solved is shown in the working drawing on page 51. The centre engine is mounted across the centre truck, and transmits the power via the gears to the 'cheese wheel', to which are attached the swifts and cranks. The truck and 'cheese wheel' are Savage's ideas, the cranks may have been patented first by William Reynolds and Charles King; the platform slide has

TREATS & W.HOLMES'S

WORLD FAMED POULTRY

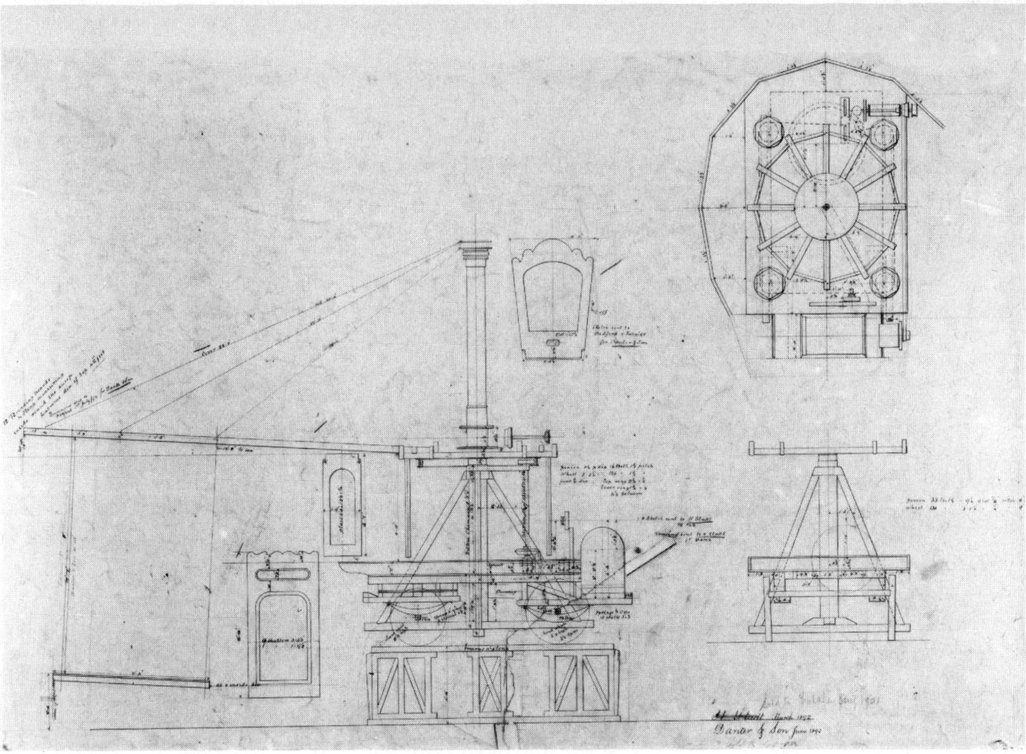

31 An early set of ‘Dobbies’

32 Platform Gallopers

33 The mechanism of top-motion Gallopers. The single cranks were attached on a parallel with the horizontal swifts

various claimants, but it was most probably invented by a showman called William Davies and patented later by Savage. There were of course many experiments with trial constructions, some of which gave important clues about the character of fairs by their very failure to work in that context. Interest in any area of invention is usually spasmodic, partly because there are so many problems to be solved, and partly because of the profound changes in technology which occur with increasing frequency. Frederick Savage and others began to develop the steam-powered ride in the years 1870 to 1880. From then on, there was intense activity on the part of inventors until about 1920, when radically new ideas about speed and dynamics came to the surface, and the ride itself began to assume completely new shapes like the Waltzer. All the work of these early designers is revealing, since each of them was trying to perfect existing rides or to realize dreams of new ones. The drawings in particular demonstrate the obsession of the period with movement, and show how much effort went into designing these early rides, and how many errors were made before the successful and usually simple solutions were discovered. To judge from the dates of the patents, inventors must have worked in isolation, because many inventions dealing with the same problem appeared in the same year. Perhaps this is not surprising since the interest

34 Charles Robinson 1886. This is possibly the worst of three remarkably inept methods which this inventor suggested for the control of the movement of the horses, and it defies almost any critical analysis. The drawing shows a machine that has far too many components, most of which are over-complex, thus creating many potentially weak structural points. To assemble such a ride would be a lengthy and extremely hazardous process. It takes six pages of complicated text in the patent to explain the drawing. Just the thing for reading in a storm en route to the next fair!

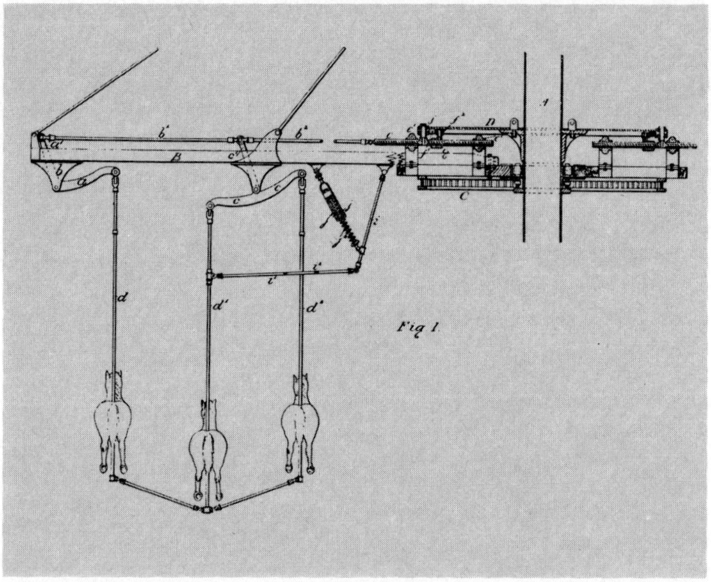

which fairground machines created attracted the attention of amateur inventors as well as engineers and showmen. So amongst the drawings on this and the subsequent pages are some that were a great success, others whose real amusement value was not the one intended by the designer!

The other major product of the 1880s and 1890s in England was the Switchback, initially built with boats or gondola cars. Among the examples illustrated on pages 54–5 are two typical Savage machines (Ills. 38, 39). The first of these is a top-motion Switchback, in which the whole of the top section moves, rather as with Gallopers, and the second is a fixed-top Roundabout with a spinning frame of 'Swifts'

35 William Reynolds and Charles King, 1886. A beautiful compromise which has the centre engine used as a small model railway, travelling in the opposite direction to the horses. The train was made to be used with platform rides also, and the speed was variable. 'C' is telescopic; 'A' is a chimney extension.

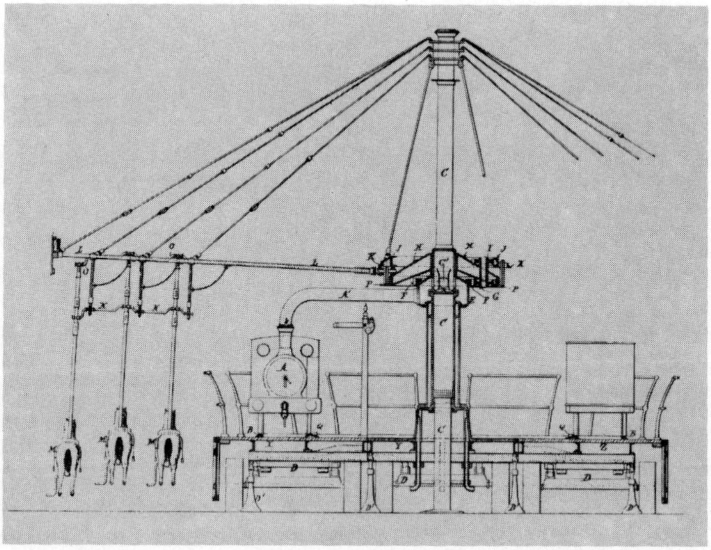

36 Henry Lake, 1894. To quote the inventor: 'The apparatus heretofore used in roundabouts for this purpose are defective inasmuch as they do not produce a galloping motion which is true to life, that is to say, the toy horse jumping with all its feet at the same time so that the front and rear part of the horse are alternately raised and lowered, while the seat, or the middle part of the horse's back moves approximately in the horizontal direction.' The 'true galloping motion' is rather out of place, and too complex. The horses would not have withstood many knocks.

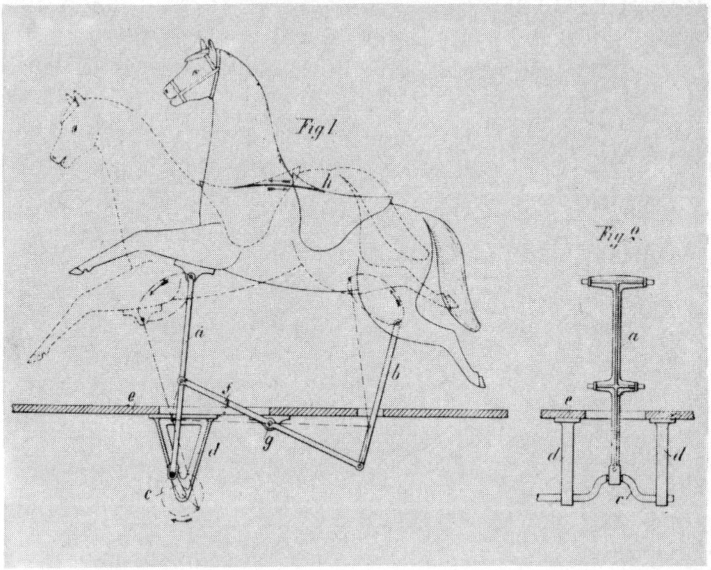

and 'Sullivans'. The whole ride would have been propelled by a centre engine, and the equipment would have included perhaps a Savage electric-light engine, an organ engine and a traction engine to pull the whole train of loads on the roads. The story of this type of ride began, as far as I can ascertain, in 1880 with the patent registered by William Sanger and Frederick Savage, containing proposals for the 'Sea-on-Land.' The invention had an arrangement of wheels and gears underneath the boat to give a 'pitching and rolling' movement, which was meant 'to resemble the movements of a vessel at sea' and the boats either had sails or were rigged like a steamer.

37 Frederick Savage and William Sanger, 1880. The support for the boat is the axis lying transversely below the centre of the bottom and connected by rods, levers and a toothed wheel to the main wheels beneath. The gears could be disengaged, and the sections separated, so that each could run on the open road on the same wheels as when the ride was in motion. The general principle of the dual purpose wheels was widely adopted since it allowed the dismantled ride to be immediately ready for transportation by road or rail, and meant a saving of many hours of unnecessary labour.

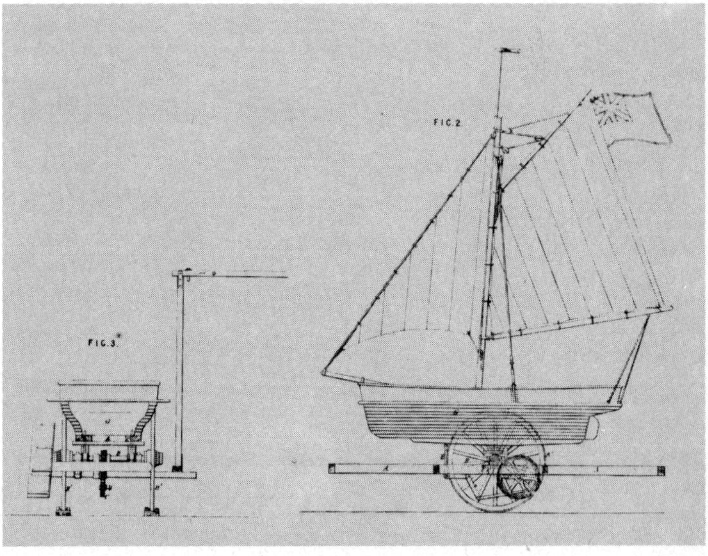

38 George Green's top-motion Switchback, 1880

39 George Twigdon's Gondola. Fixed-top Switchback, *c.* 1900

40 Gondola car from inside Percy Cole's machine, showing the attachment of the 'Sullivan' to the car

41 The centre engine of Thurston's 'Little Machine' (see page 120), 1903. Note that the engine is mounted longitudinally on the centre truck.

42 Pat Collins's steam Switchback with motor-cars, 1910

43 Holland's Dragon Switchback, at Heanor, Notts

As with the development of the 'horse' rides, many experiments were carried out with various designs before a successful version was arrived at. The kinds of activity that took place during the final two decades of the 19th century are shown in the accompanying illustrations. Only the first two are really serious propositions, or were built in any numbers. The others are clever ideas which would have proved unwieldy in practice.

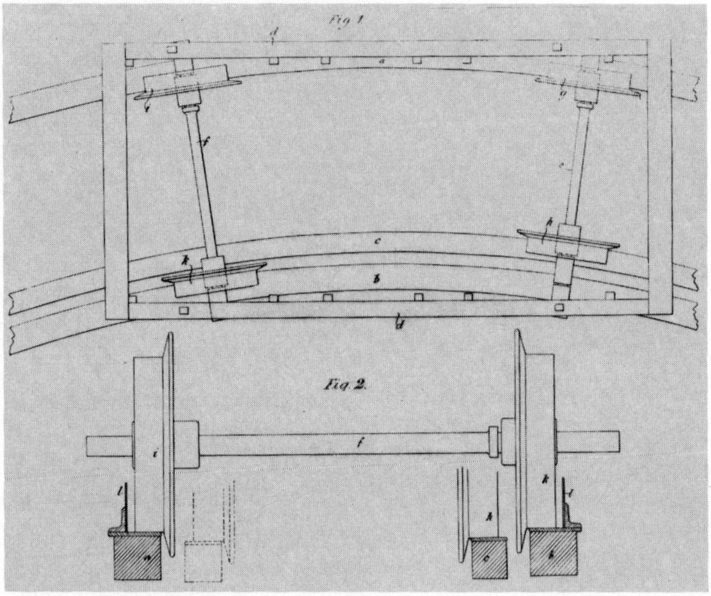

44 Frederick Savage *c.* 1888. A third compensating rail, to prevent cars leaving the tracks; a small but significant invention for the Switchback. Savage combined this with the canvas between each car to make the machines as safe as possible.

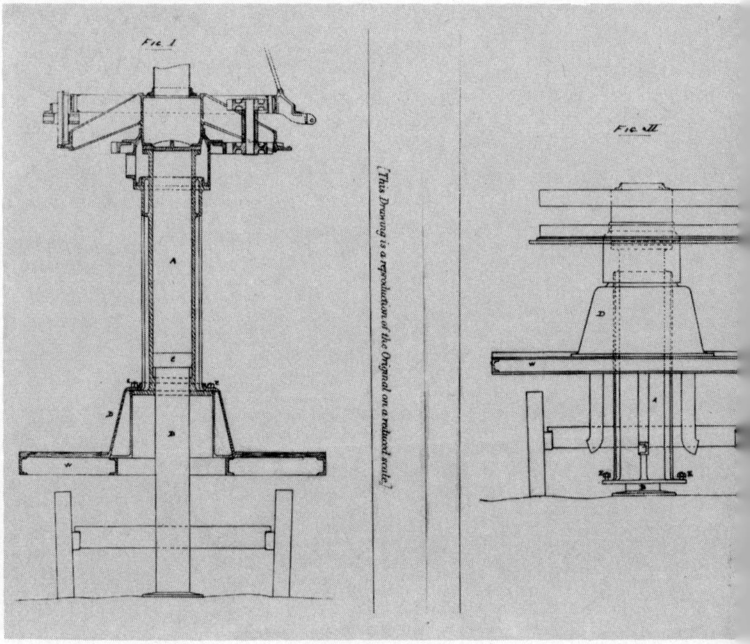

45 Frederick Burrell, 1887. The telescopic central post with a hydraulic ram was intended to travel on its own truck, thus increasing the portability of the steam roundabout. 'By the compactness produced by this arrangement the roundabout can be easily loaded upon a railway truck of the ordinary height, and be low enough to pass under railway gauges.'

Screws were sometimes used instead of water pressure.

46 William Dunkley, 1887. Plans for a 50ft portable, sectional, ride of the continuous circular pattern, with an undulating track. Proposals include the inclined track, or alternatively, inclined axles which would counteract centrifugal force when power was not supplied from a central point along connecting rods, as was usual with Switchbacks.

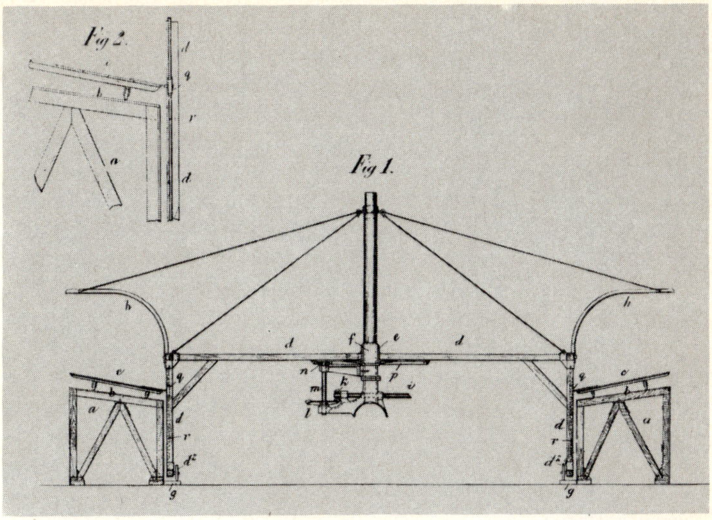

47 William Price and John Gerrard, 1887. A ride propelled in part by gravity, and part by steam or electricity. Interesting as a very early example of a proposed electric ride. Note the safety guards to prevent the cars jumping the tracks. Inside wheels are smaller than outer.

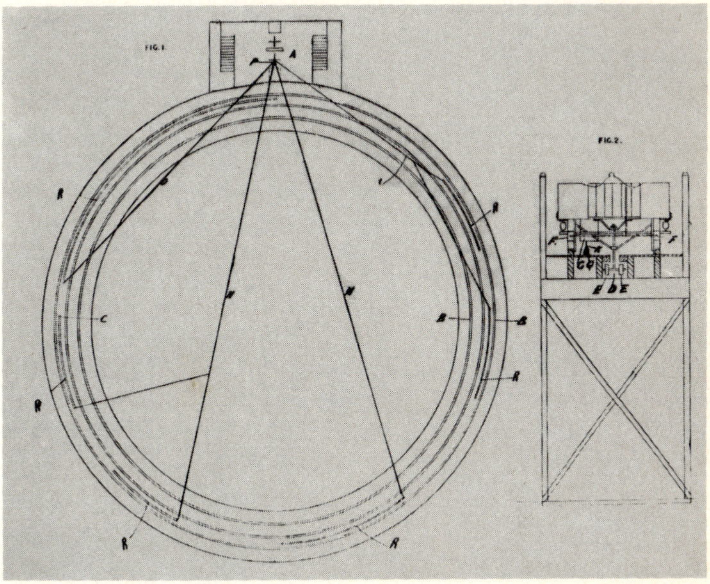

48 William West, 1887. An Archimedean Railway with a circular roofed space and spiralling track. Gravity rides, for which many of the drawings were partly intended, were not used much in this country, mainly because of the difficulty of transportation. The theoretical ideas could not be put into practice at this date because technology and materials were not sufficiently developed. The recent machines made by Anton Schwarzkopf and others are more realistic representations of the same ideas.

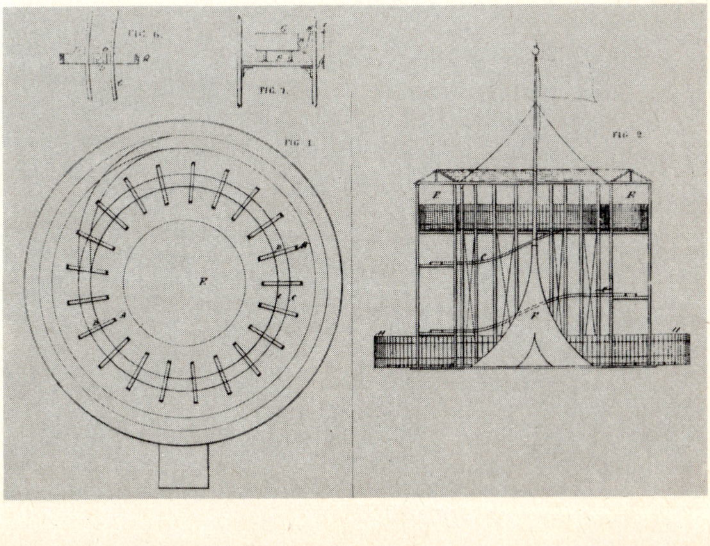

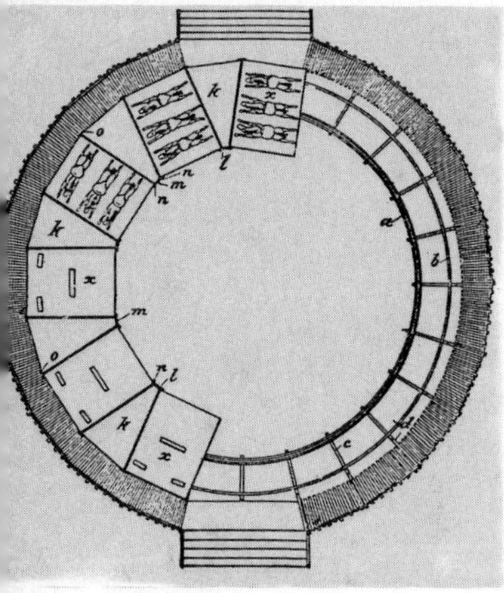

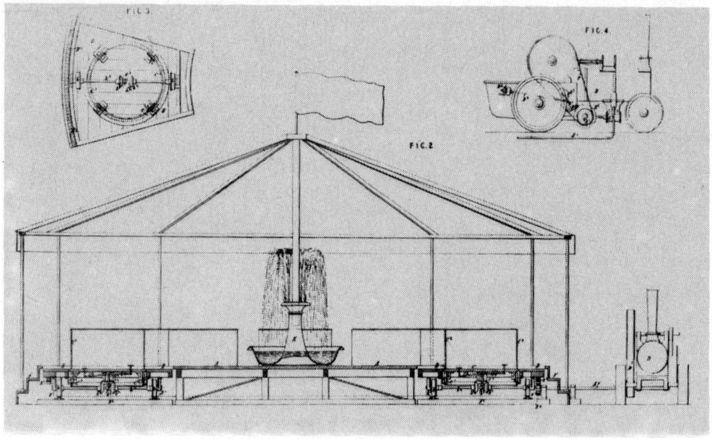

49 Everitt & Burrell's ride, forerunner of the Waltzer

50 George Green's ride, antecedent of the Noah's Ark

There are two further patents in particular which seem to derive very much from the 1880s, and which deserve more attention because in retrospect they also show clearly the origins of two much later and quite different rides. The ride proposed by Everitt & Burrell is clearly the forerunner of the now-familiar Waltzer. The cars travelled in a large circle, whilst moving to the right or left on their own axis 'after the manner of waltzers'. The centre spindle of each car had a clutch, operated by the feet of the occupants, which controlled the independent movement. The central post was there to be seized by anyone who 'felt giddy'. George Green's drawing of 1889 foreshadows the Noah's Ark which was to be the first of the new rides around 1930.

Other machines of this early period included the Tunnel Railway, the Razzle-Dazzle, and the Steam Yachts. In 1897 a steam-driven Big Wheel appeared at many northern fairs; this was followed by others at King's Lynn Mart in 1906, Stratford in 1907, and Penzance in 1911, but the real

51 The Tunnel Railway, built by Fowler of Leeds

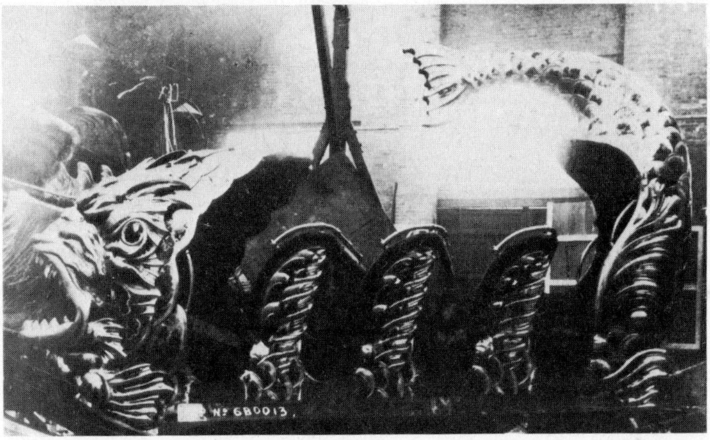

52 Scenic Whale car on test at Orton & Spooner

development of the Big Wheel occurred in America at the 'Big Eli Co.' (p. 90). In 1905 the first Helter-Skelter towers were opened by T. Harrison of Preston, Jacob Studt, and Relph & Pedley.

In 1908 Savage & Co. built their last steam-driven Switchback, for the firm of Hall & Proctor, and in 1910 came their first electrically-driven Scenic, for Enoch Farrar. With the placing of 5 h.p. electric engines under each car, the large centre engine became unnecessary; the central space could then be used for more elaborate decoration, and the showmen were free of at least one very heavy load. Opportunities for ornamentation were used in every possible way; the Italian carvers who worked for Orton & Spooner's at Burton-on-Trent, and for Savage, were given marvellous scope for their talents. The accompanying illustrations give an indication of the variety of machines produced during this period, which was inevitably short-lived, and marked the end of an era.

53 Lynn Mart, 1922. Farrer Bros building up the Scenic. The centre truck and gantry can be clearly seen; the covered objects in the foreground are two of the cars.

54 Relph & Pedley's electrically driven Motor Scenic

So far in this chapter we have been concerned with the formal history of the fairground machine, i.e. the officially registered documents, drawings and patents. Of even greater interest is the kind of 'history' which is contained only in memory and conversation; moreover there do fortunately exist some written records of the initial stages of designs in the notebooks which used to be kept by the foremen of firms like Savage & Co. The pages reproduced here come from some of these, now quite rare, notebooks of the period 1880–1910. They describe in detail the working method, including rough pencil sketches and ghosts of ideas, and show clearly that many of the suggestions for the basic arrangements of machinery, colours and structures came from the showman who was commissioning the ride. He would present his own specifications and measurements, together with a description of the number, type and size of trucks required. Drawings such as these would undoubtedly be the result of joint conversations. The notebooks also show how most fairground rides are composed of parts which have several different histories, changes to new ways of storing rides in transit, or the addition of new cars being frequent. They are believed to provide the only written record of this kind of organic design method, where engineer and showman work in close co-operation, and which is still common today.

The notes of the early 1880s contain mostly references to agricultural machinery, and a comparison of drawings will show the similarity of the mechanics. With the introduction of the fairground machine the urgency of the writing increased, due to the larger number of orders. Greater emphasis had to be placed on time, as new machines, whole or in part, would have to be complete by the date on which the fair, say Lynn Mart or Nottingham Goosefair, was due to

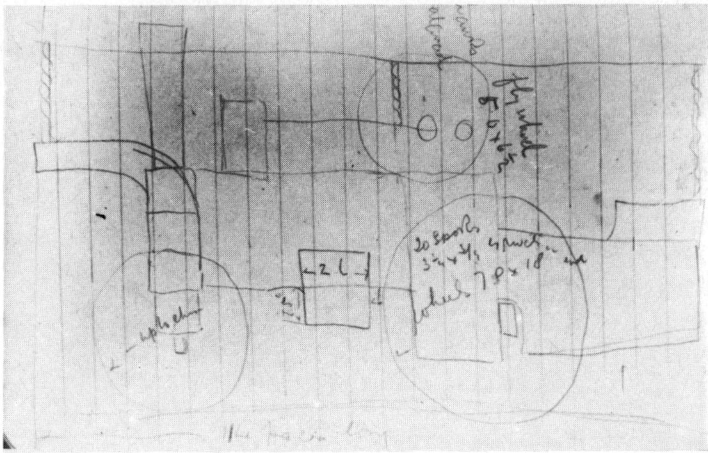

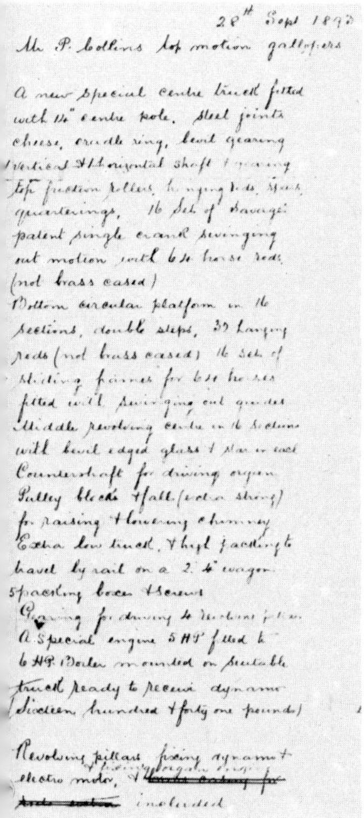
28th Sept 1893
Mr P. Collins top motion gallopers

A new Special centre truck fitted with 14" centre pole. Steel joints cheese, cradle ring, bevil gearing vertical & horizontal shaft & gearing top friction rollers, hanging rods, spars, quarterings, 16 Sets of Savage's patent single crank swinging out motion with 64 horse rods (not brass cased)
Bottom circular platform in 16 sections, double steps, 32 hanging rods (not brass cased) 16 Sets of sliding frames for 64 horses fitted with swinging out guides
Middle revolving centre in 16 sections with bevil edged glass & star in each
Countershaft for driving organ
Pulley blocks & fall (extra strong) for raising & lowering chimney
Extra low truck, & tarpaulins packing to travel by rail on a 2' 6" wagon.
5 packing boxes & screws
Gearing for driving to machine fitted
A Special engine 5 HP fitted to 6 HP. Boiler mounted on suitable truck ready to receive dynamo
(Sixteen hundred & forty one pounds)

Revolving pillars fixing dynamo & electro motor, & ~~[illegible]~~ included

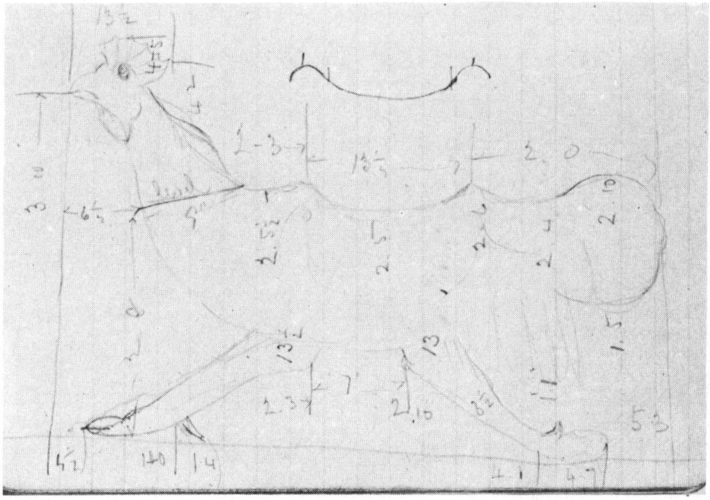

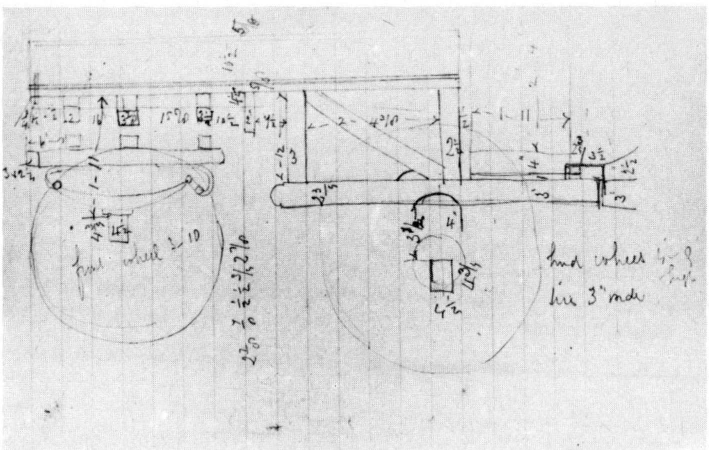

55–60 A selection of typical drawings and writings from Savage's notebooks. Slight though the drawings are, they did serve an important function in the first stages of the design of individual machines and decorations.

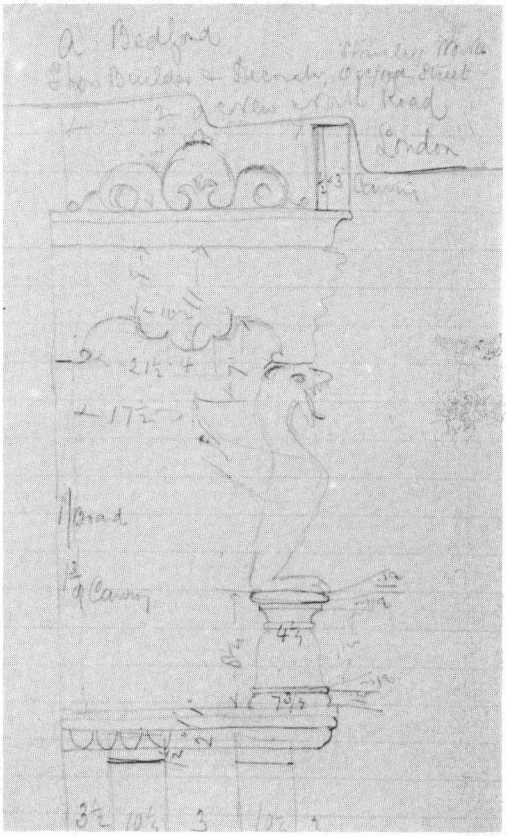

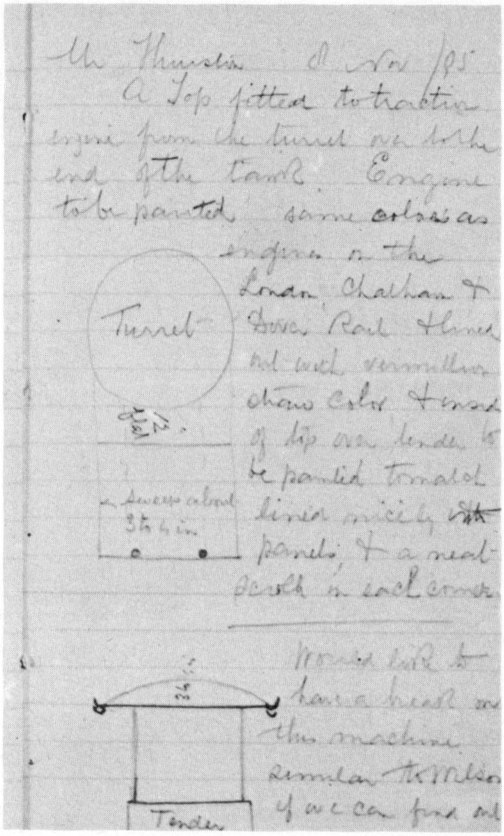

open. Most of the well-known showmen of the time are mentioned: Tuby, Thurston, Pat Collins, John Collins, Steppe, Studt and many others, each of them, as their descendants are now, very much aware of what their business rivals were up to, and quick to realize which of the new developments were worth including in their shows or machines. Parts from rides might need replacement for a variety of reasons; sometimes because they had ceased to function correctly, or perhaps a new decorative style was needed, or a new material had proved more efficient. Extracts from the notebooks of Charles Rix, at the time foreman at Savage & Co., follow and show how a fairground machine can be separated into its components and remade as a new machine, largely from informal discussion.

In February 1894 John Collins was at King's Lynn Mart with his Gallopers, and wanted some alterations ready for the final day and his next journey. Rix noted:

Feb 19th 1894 John Collins

Middle row of hanging rods are to be made whole instead of in two pieces at once ready for when he pulls down.

These changes were only minor, but later in May of the same year Pat Collins wanted the major restructuring of his set of Gondolas. He had obviously seen a similar ride owned by a French showman, M. Opitz, and was asking for copies of what he had seen. The mention of india-rubber tyres must be one of the earliest, and Savage would certainly have had to search for a manufacturer; but more significant is the suggestion that the engine from a set of galloping horses should be fitted with a new mechanism to suit the existing driving top of the Gondolas:

> Entrance to Gondolas to be lowered one foot at bottom of hill.
> To be done at once.
> New main frames.
> Three new trams.
> New walking platforms as there are two steps to mount onto cars.
> Driving wheels steel tyre as usual.
> Three wheels to have India rubber tyres.
> New walking platforms to be square frame as Gondolas.
> See where rubber tyred wheels are made. Three or four places and Mr S. will go and see them.
> Cars to be similar to Opitz, all with canopy in centre. This canopy is to be high enough to clear people's heads well. Cars to be 4 ft wide.
> Main frames to be same height as present Gondolas and walking platform to be 1 ft lower all round and extra step all round.
> See if we can make bogey to run up on rails to carry cars across it – or a curved arrangement to run up.
> Use engine out of present Galloping horses. New driving top to suit Gondolas, use all iron work possible and present Sullivans and make [brace?] to clear organ as Hobbs.
> Give Mr Collins length of twisted brass for coupling rods between frames and canvas made as soon as possible so he can have them painted.
> Six of our improved spring boxes [illegible].
> Canvas a little longer and stronger.
> Want length of boards for driving top sent on as soon as possible.
> Use present fitted top, engine, packing and chimney.
> New driving top to be painted gold colour (yellow as near to gold as possible) lined red and green. No stencils, struts and levers to be chamfered and picked out red or green. Cars to be bevelled on outside slightly.
> Wanted a week before August Bank holiday.
> Outside steps from top of hills as other Gondolas.

On February 14 of the following year Jacob Studt specified an even more complex cannibalization of equipment.

Basically the request was in two halves, the first dealing with the remaking of a 'Wheely Whirley' machine, the exact nature of which is obscure, and the second describing the rebuilding of a Switchback, using an interchange of parts from both machines. Once again the order is to a deadline:

> *14th February, 1895*
>
> 4 h.p. engine to be taken out of Switchback and put into Wheely Whirley again and all the slow motion gear refitted to crank shaft bracket and the old Wheeley Whirley cheese refitted. The two planks for the engine to stand and to be made new as the others were put into the Switchback.
> Three wagons, trams and fittings to be made for loading up Wheely Whirley tables and gear.
> 4 h.p. sea on land engine to be put into Switchback. Cheese off Wheely Whirley engine to be fitted to this engine, engine to be raised as packing to carry cheese same height and a new chimney from cheese to first joint 8′ 7″ long as Mr Studt has lengthened his present chimney 10 inches.
> Engine raised by pulling a $3\frac{1}{2}''$ plant next to the ground under the present engine packing.
> $12' 9'' \times 12' 3\frac{1}{2}''$ and the two stretchers to give right width, and collar bolts to fasten them to other packing.
> He has the scotchs for the hind wheels.
> Order to follow in rotation.
> Wanted as soon as possible.

Savage & Co. must have been a busy place, because a week and four other orders later came two equally urgent orders for alterations to Gallopers:

> *21st February*
>
> Danter wants estimate for converting his 36 horse Reynolds' motion into 56 horse Reynolds' motion, use cranks and all iron we possibly can.
>
> *21st February*
>
> Wilmot wants estimate for altering his machine into our present single crank, swinging out motion with slides in his present platform. New Bevel wheel pinions and cranks and horse irons. 3″ twisted brass to horse irons. Howcroft made platform and we are to give him separate price of altering same.

For a typical quotation from these books it would be hard to find a better example than George A. Aspland's brisk order for alterations to two of the trucks which transported his Gondolas. This would have been the sort of record that would have accompanied the drawings in Ills 56–60, and the important point is that these changes were an everyday sort of occurrence. 'Tombland fair' relates to the present Norwich Easter Fair discussed in chapter 2.

19th March 1895

Geo. Aspland here and ordered two wagons for Gondola cars to be altered.
All road wheels to be made 1′ lower and 2″ to be taken off hind and front carriage blocks.
Engine truck wheels to be rectified. Man will give instructions when he comes in a day or two.
To be done at once for Tombland fair.

Another entry reads:

Mr Thurston. November 1895

A top fitted to traction engine from the turret over to the end of the tank? Engine to be painted same colour as engines on the London, Chatham and Dover Rail and lined out with vermilion and straw colour and inside of top over tender to be painted to match, lined nicely with panels and a neat scotch in each corner.
Would like to have a [illegible] on this machine similar to Wilson if we can find out what it is, to be made and sent – wants cylinder bored as large as possible to give more power.
One spoke of hind wheel is broken – to be mended similar to the next one to it.
See to crank shaft perhaps wants lining in the brasses.
Boiler cladding to be set right and asbestos used with it;

Thurston
Circus Proprietor,
Stansted,
Essex.

Twisted brass on upright for top.

Orton & Spooner of Burton-on-Trent, no doubt collaborating with showmen as Savage did, made many fine Scenics, and later some wonderful Noah's Arks and Dodgems, but they also did most of the carved work on the Bioscope Show fronts, and on the organs which were so much a part of the fairground scene. The first exhibition of animated pictures in London took place in February of 1896 at the Polytechnic, and from this date until 1914 showmen took the films to people all over Great Britain. There were no established picture houses, nor was there any suitable means of transport for the public, so naturally the cinemas themselves had to travel! The first one to do so was owned by Randall Williams, and went as part of his Ghost Show. Often the menageries, waxworks, and marionette shows

61–63 Early shows and cinema. Electrograph Show (61); Parker's Geniis and Goblins Show, *c.* 1890 (62); Caddick's Royal Studio, *c.* 1900 (63)

were the only entertainments with enough space to display films (by 1901 Chipperfield's were showing pictures of the Boer War), and cinemas therefore began their history alongside the other illusions of the fair. The first small 'theatres' held only 50 to 60 people, and were known as 'ground booths'. Many showmen made their own films and there are reports of 'takes' in the streets of Bury St Edmunds and other small towns. Pictures would be made of the local inhabitants, who became the first generation to see themselves as glittering moving images!

At first the light used for projection purposes was produced by allowing a stream of lighted hydrogen to play onto a lime cone for a while, then turning on the oxygen gradually. The large lamps sometimes fastened to the outside of the booths are naphtha flare lamps, comprising a container holding about one gallon of oil and an iron burner heated by a small fire. By 1900 electric light and the portable steam engines made possible the complete lighting

of both inside and out, and the lime cone projector was superseded by a carbon-burning arc lamp which gave a much brighter picture. These great double-fronted shows often had seating accommodation for as many as 600, and standing room for another 400. The engines, lamps, electric light engines, 'paraders' and performers made an impressive front to these glorious shows. The mighty steam engines used for hauling made possible the heavy loads and long journeys; without them the decoration and flamboyance would have been impractical, and simply could not have happened. Sometimes pulling seven or eight trucks, they would cover distances of 250 miles or more at average speeds of 5 m.p.h., at a time when most country people did not venture more than five miles from their homes.

The showman's engine in its more recognizable form had made its appearance by 1900, complete with dynamo, smoke extension bracket, winch, canopy, twisted brass supports, and the colourful lining and painting. After 1918 many

64 Example of an early steam engine used by showmen before their own distinctive models were introduced

65 Thurston's famous Burrell 'Victory'

Scenic engines had the 'crane' added to the rear for lifting the cars. The principal manufacturers were Fowler (Leeds), Foster, Marshall and Burrell. Illustration 64 shows a forerunner of the true showman's engine, of which Thurston's 'Victory' (above) is a fine example. Fowler produced an engine in 1886 which without its canopy and in general appearance will have been similar to the early example.

Although these engines are now 'old-fashioned' they were when built many decades ahead of their time, and in concept and reality they are still very startling as a combination of steam power and electricity. They were the first wholly mobile producers of electrical power, and the showmen who drove them were the first to bring electricity to many of the gas-lit towns and villages of Great Britain. They also make an interesting study in the economics of fashion. Twenty years ago, such an engine would be sold or auctioned for about £28, but the same engine, restored and decorated, would now be beyond price – and not for antiquarian reasons alone.

Until the late 1930s many fairs continued to rely upon the steam engine for power, and the horse was not without its uses either. Diesel and petrol engines finally replaced steam because of their greater speed, and because they did not require such lengthy preparations before a long journey. The two hours needed to 'build up steam' could be more than trying to a showman who had finished work at four o'clock in the morning, and had a journey to begin four hours later. The strength of the engines lay in their bulk, but it also made them extremely ponderous, and prone to skidding on stone surfaces or on mud. The addition of rubber or wooden tyres helped, but failed to solve the problem wholly. Water was difficult to carry in large enough

66 A. Martin & Sons' wagons and trucks passing through Hicknall hauled by their Fowler No. 8331

quantities, and finding water in darkness, in strange territory, with no moon, must have been at times rather terrifying. Add to this the pressure gauge which required constant attention, and the need to uncouple loads, to winch them separately up steep hills. The winch, with its 50 or 100 feet of steel cable, was all-important, and essential for negotiating hills, or for pulling heavily laden trucks from treacherous ground. The newer and lighter rides simply did not need so much power; the Noah's Arks were cheaper to buy than Scenics, costing hundreds instead of thousands of pounds, and were also easier to erect and dismantle. Although there were steam-powered Arks, and even Dodgems, these were soon replaced by a diesel/electric combination. Some showmen found themselves in financial trouble, having invested large sums of money on a Scenic, thinking that they would at most only need to replace the cars, as fashion changed, but the sudden advent of the new age took them by surprise. The quicker and more exciting rides sounded the death knell for the carved and gilded fantasies of old, which were sadly no longer appropriate to a period whose inspiration was to be in speed and aerodynamics. The Scenic revolved at no more than walking pace, and in the 1930s when few people had cars, they could always whizz round on an Ark for a penny! Savage & Co. built their last Scenic in 1920 for Fred Gray; Orton & Spooner continued making them for a little longer. They made dragon cars to replace the 'motor' cars from 1922, peacocks in 1923, dolphins and even geese in 1927. Their last complete Scenics were made with dolphin cars in 1926 for Jennings (Devizes) and for W. Davies.

The real impact of the newer rides began to make itself felt in the late twenties and thirties with the Ark and

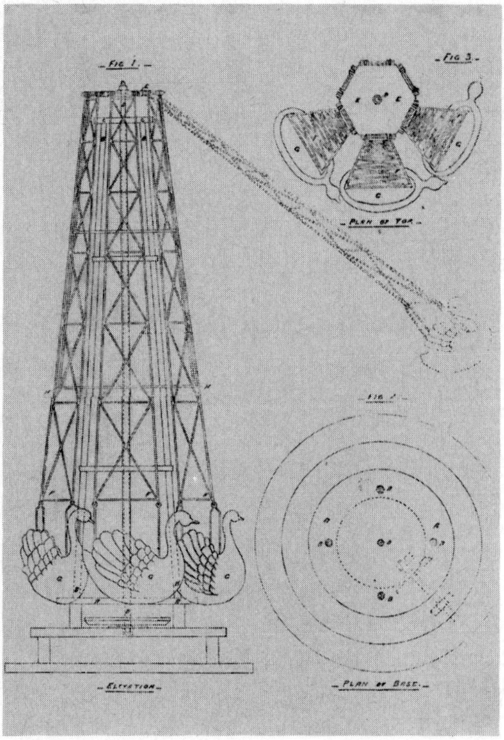

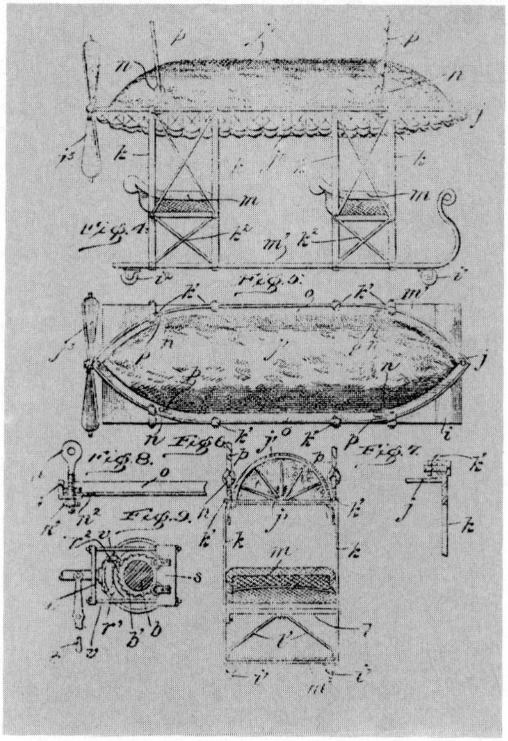

67 John Inshaw (Birmingham), 1888/9. Design for a centrifugal pleasure machine

68 Rudy Uzzell (Denver, Colorado), 1904. Design for swinging chairs

Waltzer, but indications of the way things were moving could be detected in earlier designs. The Everitt & Burrell idea of a Waltzer was of sedately revolving platforms, moving, as you might expect, 'after the manner of waltzers'. The 20th-century interpretation was as far removed from the Viennese Waltz as can be. The machine became something fast and exciting, and the dance turned into more of a whirl! Decoration was sharper, flatter, and colours were stronger. For the first time one finds in the patent specifications phrases like 'exhilaration attendant upon the increased speed'.

Rides patented well before 1920 already showed signs of these new preoccupations, when they began to come to Great Britain from Europe and America. The Chairoplanes of 1888 by John Inshaw are surprising because they must have been one of the first machines, if not *the* first, capable of giving the sensation of sustained powered flight! The Wright brothers did not succeed with powered flight until 1903, some 15 years later, and the Chairs were a kind of amusing but prophetic response to the growing interest in flying. Rudy Uzzell's patent of 1904 for a set of swinging chairs is a curious bridge between the world of 19th-century fiction and the aeroplanes which were to dominate the coming age. The notion is modern, but the cars look as though they were constructed from a plan made by Jules Verne. The central post is essentially a giant maypole, and the cars

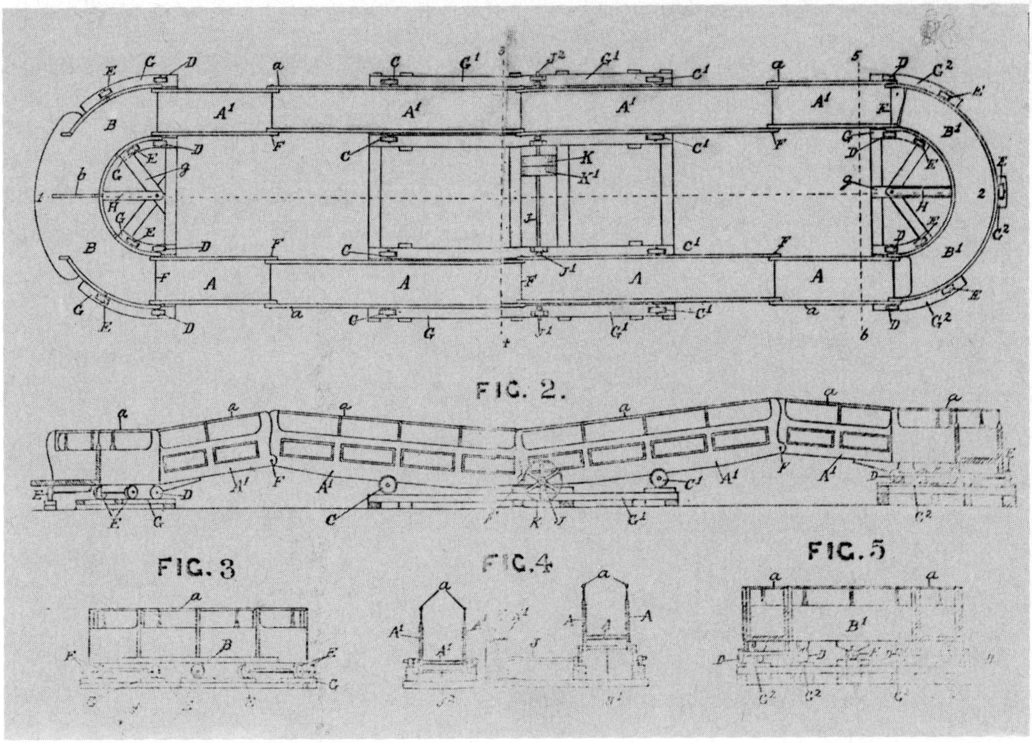

69 Herbert Lawson (Cleethorpes), 1909. The Cakewalk. On the first appearance of this ride an enthusiastic reporter wrote: 'You may be the most ungraceful and elephantine person in the world, but once you get on this mechanical bucking mule, your worst enemy would be forced to say that for gracefulness and the poetry of motion in general, Pavlova, Karsavina, and the whole Imperial Russian Ballet are among the also ran.'

have ornithological rather than mechanical origins. A lot of showmen bought later and smaller models of Chairoplanes from Germany in the 1920s when exchange rates were rather more satisfactory than they are today. Frank Sedgwick Snr had a set without a platform, which was clumsy to transport, and difficult for passengers to mount or dismount. He cut the central column and constructed a platform, making the ride more like the Chairs we know now.

The ungraceful but compelling Cakewalk has its beginnings in George Tilyou's almost surreal moving staircase of 1902. The ideas were taken up by Walter Taylor and Herbert Lawson in 1907 and 1909. In 1907 the 'Brooklyn Cakewalk' was travelled by the patentees, and by Easter 1908 there were three of them at Wanstead Flats. In 1914 William Mangels from Brooklyn USA made his proposals for the ride which came to be known as the 'Whip'. The new aesthetic was now clear, as this futurist quotation attests:

> Each car will travel along the straight portions of the track and acquire a quick centrifugal motion in passing around the curves, turns or corners, the suddenness of which causes agitation or commotion of the occupants, and hence much merriment and amusement!

This was of course the 'daddy' of the Swirl, and the first of the 'excitement' machines.

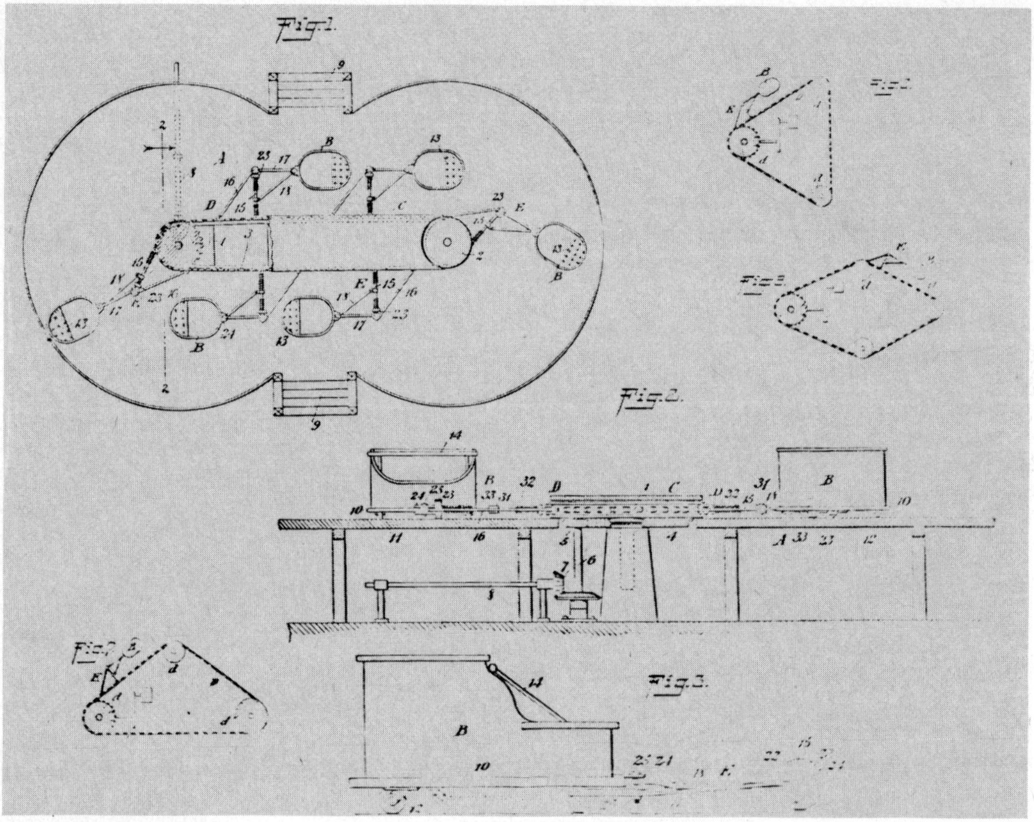

70 William Mangels, U.S.A., 1914. The Whip

The waltzing idea made its reappearance as a drawing in 1919, in the form of specifications submitted by Dennis Jeffrey and Herbert Jackson. Not until ten years later in 1929 did Thomas Jackson devise the Waltzer which most of us recognize. Any memories of the graceful pirouettes suggested by Burrell are dispelled by the exciting and powerful proposals put forward here. The word 'waltz' is in fact absent from the textual description, and the words 'oscillate' and 'swing' are used instead. One of the differences between the drawing reproduced in Ill. 71 and the later rides which are now on the roads, is that '18' and '19' are now affixed to 4″ × 8″ laminated wood, to be separate from the track, thus allowing easier building of the machine. The centre construction has also slightly altered.

In the same year, 1929, John Thurston and Robert James Lakin[1] patented the Swirl in Great Britain. By 1930 the Noah's Arks were being made here; Maxwell's built one, another was bought new from Orton's by Silcock Bros, and travelled with Burrell No. 3334 'The Bardie'.

In 1933 Lakin and Charles Thurston redesigned the Waltzer. The first machine, built in that year, was delivered to Charles Thurston and went into service, still in-

1 Bob Lakin was for many years a skilled craftsman with Orton & Spooner.

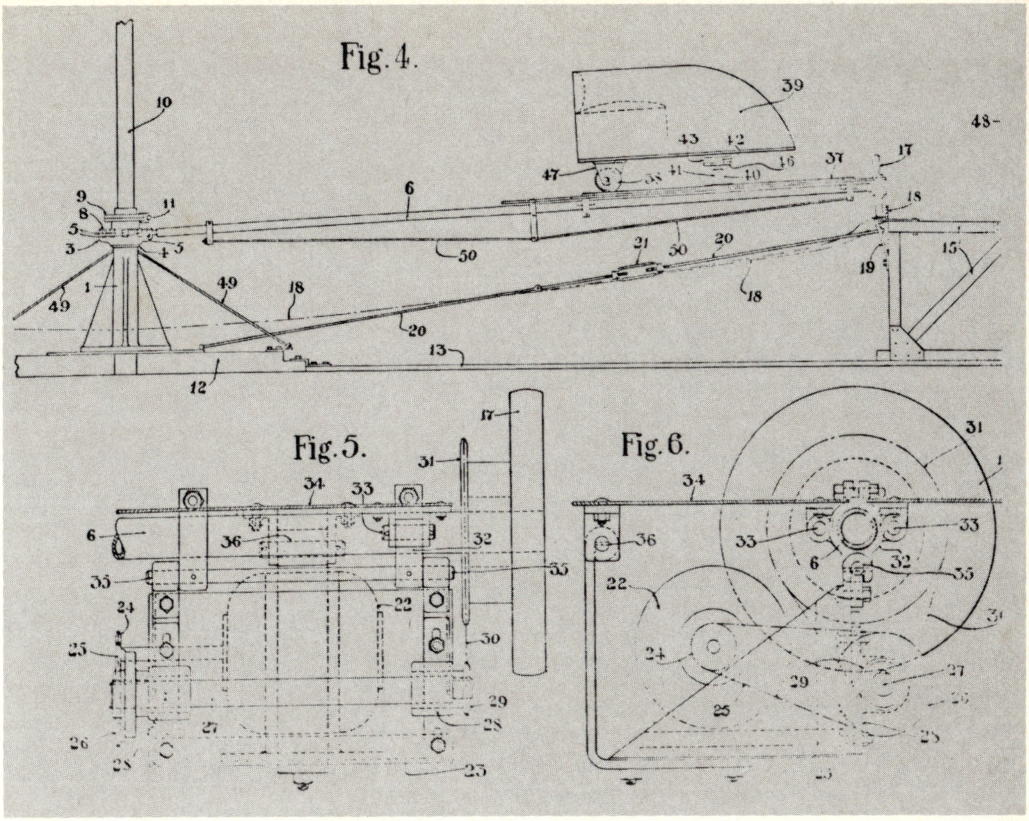

71 Thomas Jackson (Lancaster), 1929. The Waltzer

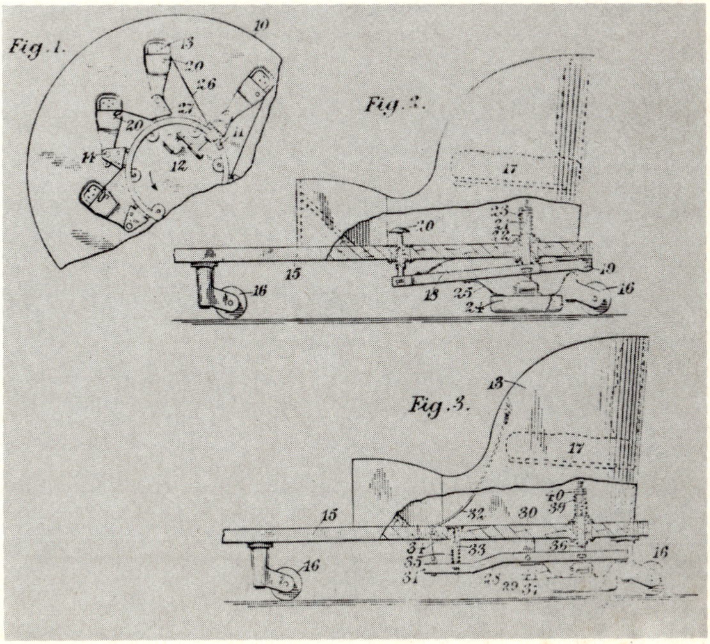

72 John and Charles Thurston (Norwich) and James Lakin (London), 1929. The Swirl

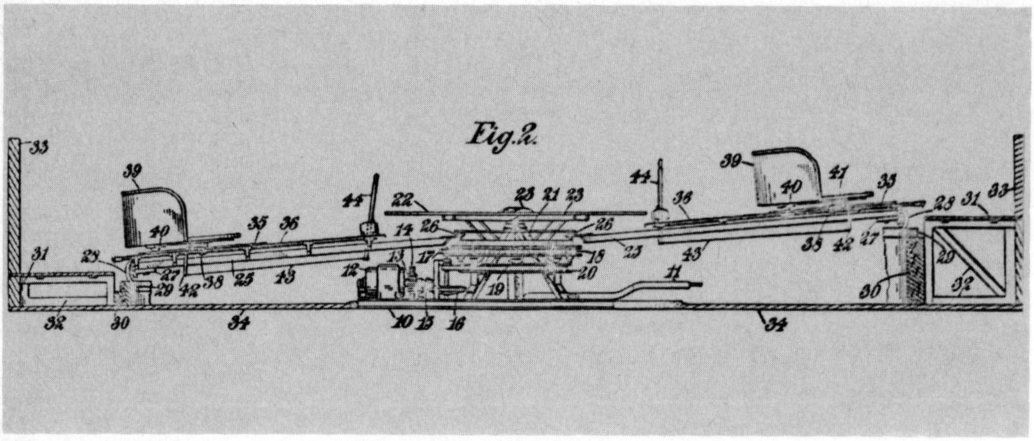

73 James Lakin and Charles Thurston, 1933. The Waltzer

complete, at Bush Hill from the 28th to the 31st July. The designers had added a brake to this ride to give 'an element of surprise':

'The car will rotate through 180° with respect to the flooring and the character of such rotation will depend upon the degree of friction in the axle and the rollers of wheels, and such factors as the gradient of the track, and the degree of eccentricity of the centre of gravity of each car; and any desired effect, such as a sudden jolt, may be produced by suitable co-ordination of these factors.'

The cheese wheel of the Waltzer is largely unchanged *in principle* from the one which Savage designed for Switchback or Gallopers (see page 42).

Machines based on Tom Orton's ideas of 1935 for an inclined track proved relatively unsuccessful, although some 'Moon Rockets' are still travelling. The angle of the ride creates enormous pressure on the high wall of the machine, which required therefore a slow and careful build-up of its very heavy components. The 'Octopus', with all its variations owes a lot to Lee Eyerley's patent of 1936. The 'Dive Bomber', also a product of the Eyerley Aircraft Co. (Oregon), was patented in England in April 1940. Eyerley began his career by designing flight simulators for pilot training and experimenting with contemporary aerobatic ideas. As for the Rotor of 1949, the very idea sounds terrifying:

'Persons standing inside the cylinder as the bottom surface of the same, are forced against the wall of the cylinder and are held there, fast by the centrifugal force occurring during the rotation of the cylinder.'

There are several of these spectator-orientated rides travelling the country, but centrifugal force seems rather to have lost all innocence—witness the Wall of Death or the even more extraordinary Globe of Death!

The number of patents relating to the Dodgem car is an indication of the success of this ride over many years. One

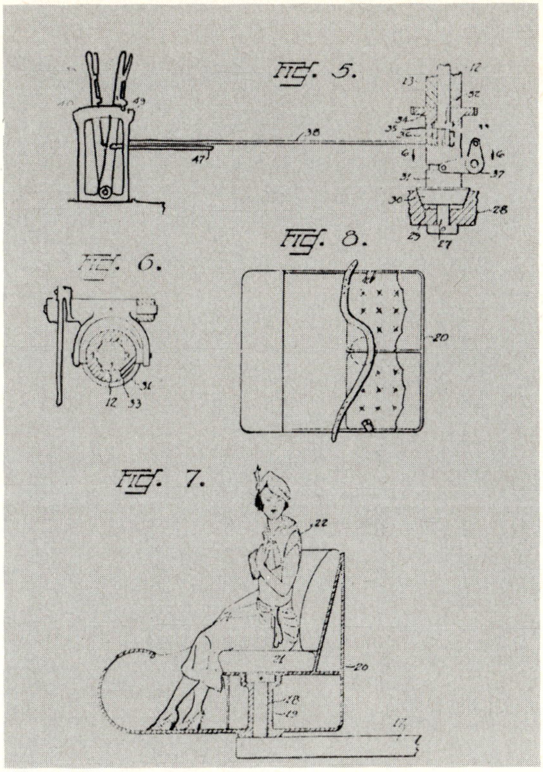

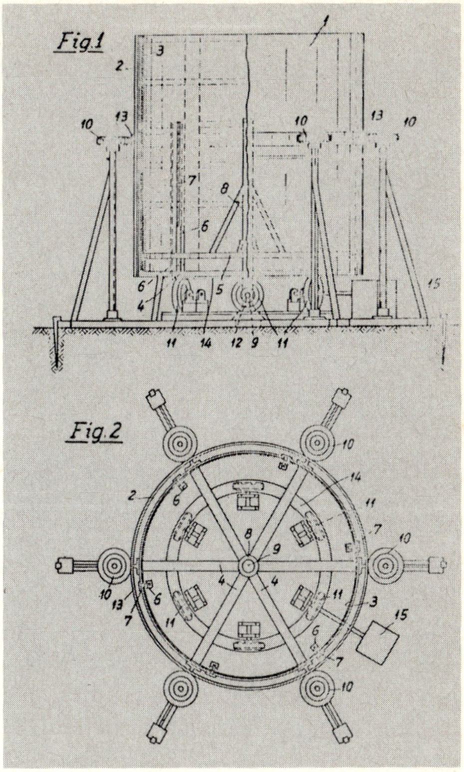

74 Lee Eyerley (Salem, Oregon), 1936. A car from his original drawing for the Octopus. The lady doesn't seem fully prepared for the journey which awaits her; to hold so elegant a pose on an Octopus, even in 1936, would require more than the will to do so.

75 Ernst Hoffmeister (Eben, Bavaria), 1949. 'Improvements relating to a rotating cylinder for amusement purposes' (the Rotor)

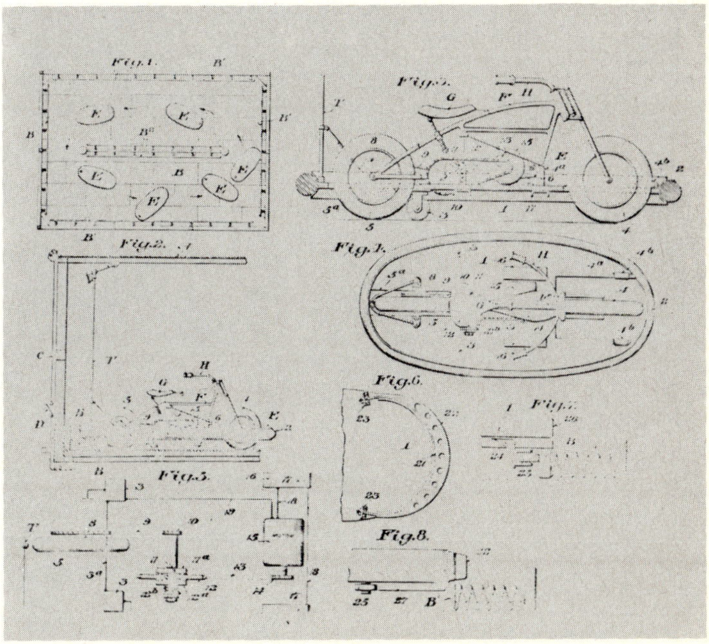

76 F. L. Markey and H. Stoehrer (U.S.A.), 1936. Design for a Dodgem car

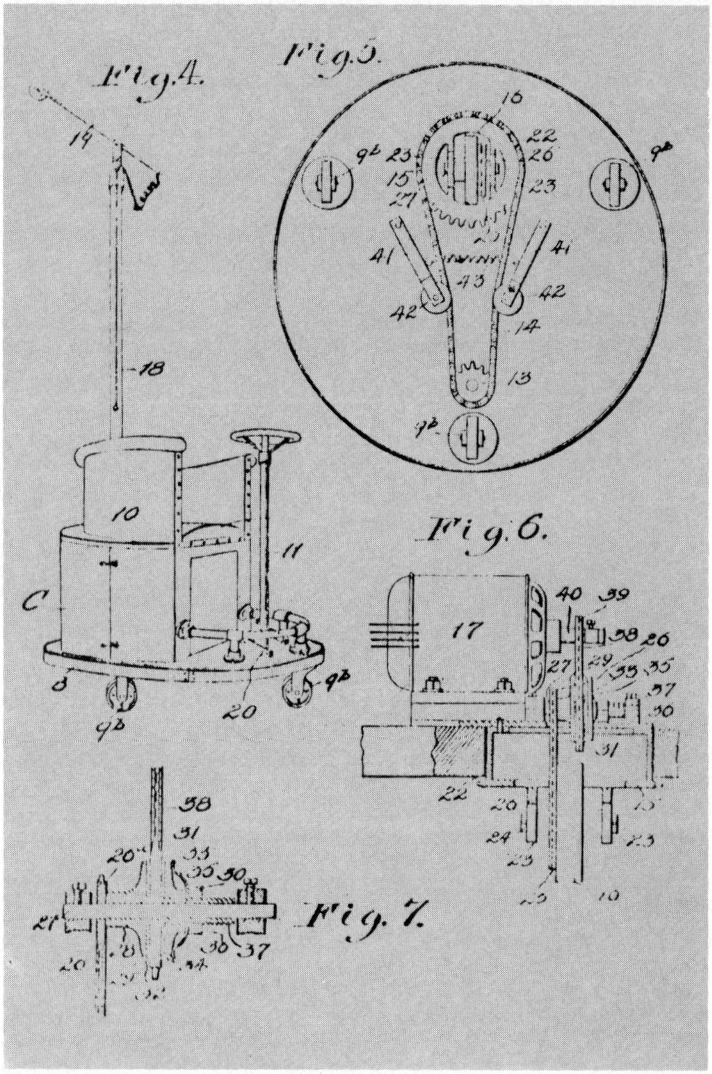

77 M. and H. Stoehrer (Mass., U.S.A.), 1922. Dodgem car

of the first tracks belonged to the firm of Bolesworth, and appeared on Wanstead Flats at Easter 1928. Like most sets of the time it had an organ in one corner, and was square in plan. Since then both tracks and cars have undergone enormous changes in style and structure as can be seen by a comparison of Ills. 76 and 87.

This chapter has covered in general outline fairground rides from their beginnings to the design of some of the basic modern rides, but this isn't the end of the story. Manufacturers are constantly improving the design of wagons and rides, and a whole new generation of equipment is coming into use.

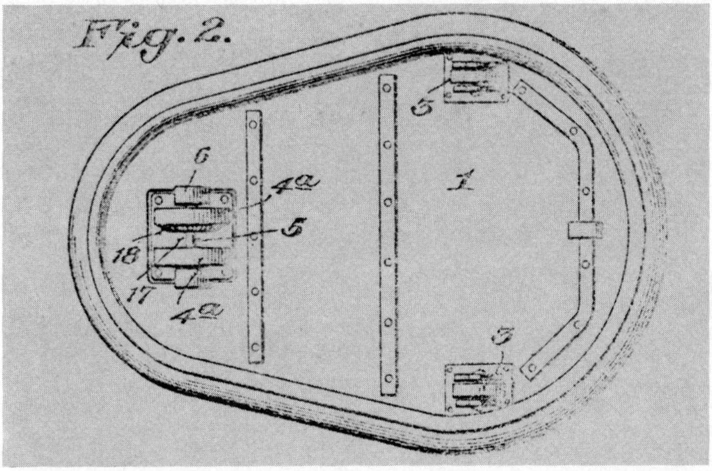

78 F. L. Markey (U.S.A.), 1931
Dodgem

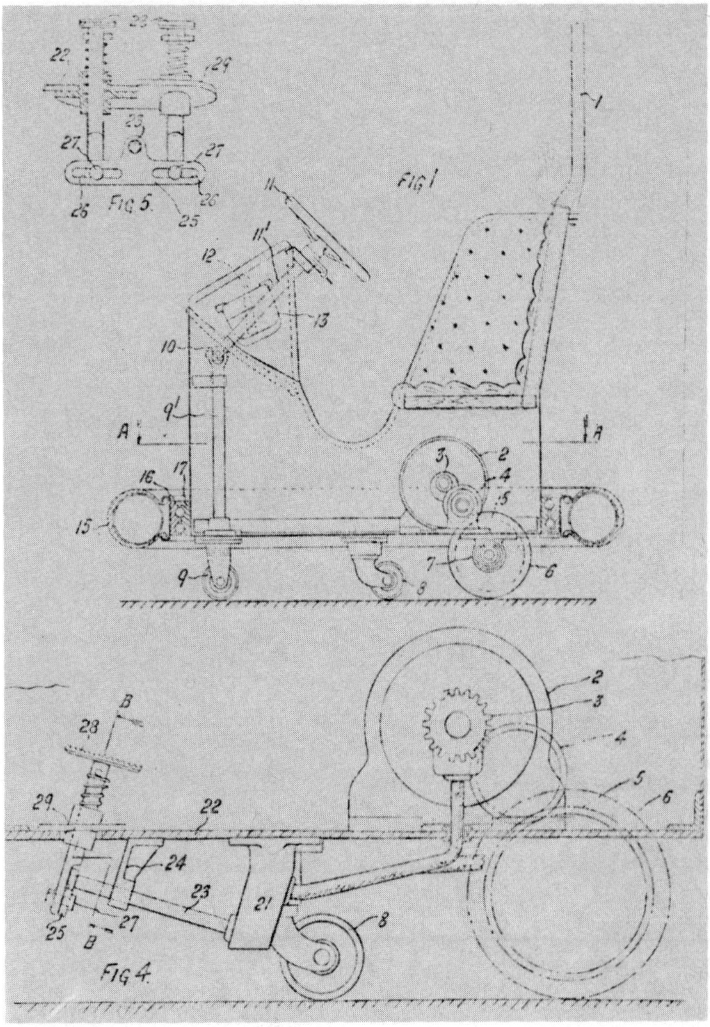

79 Celeste Capitelli (U.S. citizen living in London), 1926. Dodgem car

WORLD'S MOST
EXCITING RIDE
THE
A SPACE

4 THE NEW MANUFACTURERS

80 The Folding Round-Up. Height 42 ft, operating space 40 ft square. Diameter of wheel 29 ft. Weight 27,000 lb. Passengers stand around the circumference, facing the centre. The wheel is rotated at 18½ r.p.m. and generates enough centrifugal force to allow the wheel to be tipped at an angle of 70 degrees. (Hrubetz)

The development of the fairground ride did not stop in 1930, nor are fairs dying out; only the invention, decoration and music are of a different kind. The machines remain basically circular, but have their inspiration in speed, in the exploration of space, and in the movement of planets, rather than in mythical beasts, horses and gondolas. New myths have replaced the old, and the ways in which they find expression, with the use of new as well as the more traditional materials, are very exciting. Change is after all inevitable and indeed has always been the most integral part of fairground life, even if this has meant a reversion to older methods and materials when modern ones became no longer viable.

Savage & Co. and Orton & Spooner Ltd were among the first well-known manufacturers. Neither of these firms now make rides, and Savage's have unfortunately closed down completely. J. R. Lakin, and Langwheels, who made many of the early Waltzers, Swirls and Jets between 1930 and the late 1950s have also gone out of business. Firms currently building equipment in Great Britain for fairs include H. P. Jackson, a very old-established firm, and one of the originators of the Waltzer; George Maxwell Ltd, who built some of the first Noah's Arks; Supercar Ltd, Whittaker Bros, Bennett's Amusement Co., and several well-known makers of wagons.

Many new and remarkable machines now travelling in this country were made in America or Europe, and a comparison of the different manufacturers throughout the world shows that designs can vary significantly according to their country of origin. The Big Wheels made in America, in Germany and in Great Britain differ from each other in type and character, and these differences will be clear from the illustrations. Some of the American rides in particular look rather bare compared with the machines decorated either by English showmen or by firms of professional decorators like Hall and Fowle (p. 38). To eyes used to Maxwell's glorious Waltzer (p. 85) the American equivalent seems unimaginative, and the 'plastic' Carousel is no match for the genuine carved Gallopers (pp. 40–2). On the other hand the rides which were initiated and developed entirely in America, such as the Octopus, are quite startling. The fact that the ride is appropriate in shape and character to its background gives it an aesthetic quality.

The initial advance of European and American patents into the British market has already been discussed in the previous chapter. It is sometimes said that the rides built in Britain by Langwheels, J. R. Lakin, Maxwell's and others were responsible for the closure of Savage's and the older firms. Savage & Co. relied too heavily upon their high reputation and their out-dated methods of production, failing to see the newer opportunities. So the wooden patterns remained unused and covered with dust for many years, until they were recently sold to become part of a museum. There is no doubt that the firm could have remained in production, and the misfortune is that there is a new market for Gallopers, and the sort of rides which Savage's used to build. One has the feeling that Frederick Savage himself would not have let slip such an opportunity!

One of the basic reasons for the difference in the style between American and English machines is the fact that when Savage was making steam-powered electricity-producing engines in the early 1900s, Eli Bridge and other companies on the far side of the Atlantic were experimenting successfully with petrol-driven models; the greater speed and compactness that these offered gave rise to a different kind of aesthetic. There are other obvious cultural differences reflected in phenomena like the development of Jazz, and the growth of Hollywood in America, and these too may have prompted or made possible the sharper style. The American ride would appear to have grown directly out of the 20th century, instead of evolving from a very long tradition of performing arts and seems above all else to be based on machines like the aeroplane or the bobsleigh, rather than on a history of ideas about dances or of animal movements. The European firms have for the most part been founded more recently than their British counterparts, and have taken their design initiative from the American and more immediately contemporary styles.

There follow brief particulars of the leading makers of fair equipment of the present time, accompanied by illustrations of some of the magnificent rides they manufacture, beginning with Great Britain. For the technically-minded specifications are given, in order to help elucidate particular aspects of these rides, the background to which varies fundamentally according to nationality. Standardization of information is difficult because of the differences in design and conception. Unless otherwise stated, these modern machines are all transportable, being either trailer-mounted or built around uniform-sized container units.

GREAT BRITAIN

The history of the British fairground stems largely from the complementary involvement of individual showmen and engineers in design, much more so probably than else-

81 Exterior of wagon built at the turn of the century

where in the world. The story of the development of the wagon in Britain is typical of this type of system. The freight and living wagons are the heart of travelling fairs; showmen apparently had wagons very early in the 19th century, before Romanies adopted them, and seem to have initiated the design themselves. The early horse-drawn wagons, 12 to 16 feet long, were frequently built by the owners, sometimes on the road between fairs. The patterns seem to have derived partly from farm wagons, and later to have been influenced by the railways when showmen used to send the heavier loads by rail, often building wagons and centre trucks (Ill. 45) to meet the British railway gauge requirements. There have also been several generations of professional wagon builders, including William Dunton of Reading, Howecroft, Brayshaw and, recently, Sipson and 'Colchester'.

In the 1930s John E. Mills, the founder of the eponymous firm at Colchester, was a cabinet-maker of some reputation concerned with the design of traditional English furniture. In 1937 he built for himself a holiday caravan, mainly because his regard for craftsmanship did not extend to the contemporary commercial light trailer. In 1945 he met showman Arthur Stocks, and three years later built for him a four-wheeled wagon. This marked the beginning of the development of the large and magnificent vehicles for which the firm is now famous, but the process of evolution took many years. The first type of small four-wheeled

82 Interior of wagon built at the turn of the century

83 Albert Botton's double wagon

84 Heavy six-wheeled chassis of the kind used in building a Colchester

chassis, used on Arthur Stocks' wagon, continued in use for a long time, even on the most ambitious double wagon made for Albert Botton. A close-coupled chassis with the four wheels at the centre appeared about 1958 and allowed a length of 24 to 30 feet. By 1960 a heavier four- or six-wheeled chassis came into use, and this was strong enough to allow wagons to be built up to the full legal limit of 12 metres. The main innovation in the 1960s was the articulated unit; a 37 ft ensemble was made for Harry North in 1965, and a 40 ft one for John Badell in 1967.

Each 40 ft Colchester takes the firm three and a half months to build in its small factory, and the fastest rate of production was five 32 ft wagons in one year. The craftsmanship that still goes into the making of these wagons is in the same tradition as that which has produced the best English furniture. They must be well constructed to stand

85 The Maxwell Waltzer

years of travelling over all manner of terrain, in all weathers; indeed, like most of the showmen's vehicles, they are built to last for as long as they are likely to be needed. The work of construction is done without the extensive use of plans, and only a very simple outline drawing is used. The chassis is fitted with floor platforms, the sides are built flat on this surface, the outer aluminium sheeting is cut to shape, and the inner wooden skin is fixed to the frame. When the two sides are complete, they are erected and fixed to the long sides of the chassis and floor. The ends and the roof are then fitted on, followed by the inside partitions and furnishing. Finally the outer aluminium surface, previously cut to shape, is added. Wagons built on this pattern can be seen at fairs all over the British Isles; they are a characteristic feature of the English fairground.

The travelling home of the showman is the focal point of the fair, which burgeons all round it once the fairground is reached. Soon after arrival the rides in all their colourful variety emerge from the containers like butterflies from a chrysalis, and spring into dynamic life.

George Maxwell & Son. Manufacturers of Amusement Devices. Musselburgh, Scotland.

The first machine made by the firm was a Dodgem track, built in 1929. Many were made and one was exported to Iceland. In 1930 a Noah's Ark was built, and in 1933 a fourteen-year patent was taken out on the Waltzer. Over the years the firm have produced about 170 Waltzers and they still remain one of the most popular rides. Other machines produced include Mont Blonc, The Moonrocket, The Trabant, Ferris wheel, Upright Paratrooper, Jets, Toboggan, Astroglides, and the latest, the Skyrider, a drop-down Paratrooper, which is enjoying spectacular success.

Supercar Co. (Coventry) Ltd.

This firm has been in existence since 1929, beginning in London making water Dodgems, and after moving to Coventry in 1930, specializing in Dodgems, Speedway cars and tracks. The war forced another move to Warwick, where they began to make alloy tracks, and to develop a unique light alloy base for Dodgem cars.

They now also make children's rides of all kinds, Peter Pan trains, Skyline Slides, American Coasters, and Dark Ride tracks and cars. Many of these are exported to Australia, Malaysia, India, South Africa and the U.S.A. Almost every fair in Great Britain will have as one of the main rides a set of Dodgems with a Supercar alloy track.

Recently Supercar have been renovating and reconstructing many of the tracks which they originally built many years ago. A new set of floor plates were put into John

86 A Supercar Dodgem set, recently sent to America

Murphy's Dodgems in 1972. The set was new in 1947, and was one of the first aluminium tracks made! Teddy Morley's Dodgems, over 20 years old, were also recently fitted with a square end, steps, continuous walkround with 16ft openings and glass-fibre rounding boards.

Whittaker Bros (Amusement Rides) Ltd

Predominantly manufacturers of Dodgems, although they have made Jets and many amusements for children. The company was formed in June 1945. Production of Dodgem cars began on a large scale in 1952. Until 1956 the cars were made from steel; until, that is, glass-fibre became a useful material, allowing the easy formation of a wide variety of shapes and styles. Exports now go to many countries throughout the world including Mexico, New Zealand, Norway, Turkey, Brazil and Peru.

Bennett's Amusements

Formed in 1961, the firm has made large numbers of rides during the sixties (an example is shown in Ill. 112), as the following record shows:

1961–65	24 Cyclone Twists
1965–66	9 fixed pole Paratroopers
1966–68	53 mini jets for children
1967–69	16 Trabants (one is at Great Yarmouth)
1968	A Big Wheel (for Sweden)
1969	Flying Coasters

During 1969 and 1970 Bennett's made only Astra Glides, giant slides with nine, six or four lanes, which they sent to all parts of the world.

87 The Whittaker Dodgem car. Typical of the modern type of car. The body is made of glass-fibre reinforced with steel. Headlamps: 110 volts D.C. The Motor is of the Reverchon Electric type. $\frac{3}{4}$ h.p. 110 volts. D.C. It is circular with a double shaft extension. The outer casing of the motor is fitted with a rubber tyre, and the whole casing revolves about the centre shaft. As the motor commences to revolve a clutch comes into action, and the drive is transmitted to the gear-box which is built into the motor casing. The gear-box is totally enclosed and the hardened nickel-chrome gears run in oil. Ball-bearings are of the sealed type and require no attention. Steering is by bevel gear and pinion. The base is made of steel suitably ribbed, surrounded by a pneumatic rubber bumper. Maximum speed: 8 m.p.h.

88 Schwarzkopf's steel coaster Jet Star III. Height 56 ft, operating space 108 ft by 94 ft, track 2,854 ft. Weight 167.315 tons. This is the largest of the three fully portable coasters made by this firm. The sixteen cars are coupled in pairs, each car holding six adults. The ride can be dismantled and transported easily on the 40ft containers. All the coasters are well equipped with brakes and numerous devices to prevent slipping on gradients. Schwarzkopf make two smaller models. The steel coaster Jet Star II is 45 ft high, its operating space 152 ft by 82 ft. The track is 1,919 ft long and the whole ride weighs 87 tons. The eight cars each hold six adults. The Jet Star I is 45 ft high, its operating space 144 ft by 89 ft. The track is 1,766 ft long and the ride weighs 64 tons. The ten cars each hold four passengers.

Since then they have resumed production of large machines, including hydraulic Paratroopers and the new 21-car Tri-Star. The firm has become the sole distributor of the Dodgems, Jets, etc. of the Spanish Company Perez, and make these under licence in England. Perez have a reciprocal arrangement with Bennett's in Spain.

EUROPE

In continental Europe there are many interesting companies like Perez (Spain), Reverchon (France) and Pinfari (Italy). In Germany new and adventurous rides are being manufactured by Anton Schwarzkopf. This company has been building equipment for fairs and circuses since 1955 and exporting to Russia, Canada, South America, Japan and many other countries.

Perhaps the most remarkable rides are the large Wheels, some 150ft in diameter, which recall the Giant Wheels of the 19th-century exhibitions. Another speciality seems to be the Gravity Ride, but most of the new types of machine, engineered in a beautiful and characteristic style, can be seen in this country.

89 Segments from Schwarzkopf's 51ft wheel

90 Zeppelin I. Height 79 ft, operating space 85 ft by 82 ft. Weight 89 tons. There is also a larger version 90 ft high. The five 'Zeppelins' hold twelve passengers each.

91 Some precision engineering from the Ferris Wheel showing portable components. Height 112 ft, diameter 100 ft, operating space 49 ft by 59 ft. Weight 160 tons. The ride is erected and dismantled with the aid of an electric hydraulic system. Another, smaller, portable Wheel, closer in size to the Wheels made in Britain and the U.S.A., is also produced. It is 59 ft high and 51 ft in diameter, with sixteen cars each holding six adults. The steel arms which support the ride can be seen in Ill. 89. These arms, both on the same side of the Wheel, are also raised and lowered hydraulically.

92 One of the cars for Schwarzkopf's steel Jet Star III (See Ill. 88)

93 Apollo 14. Height 79 ft, operating space 82 ft by 105 ft. Weight 140 tons. The glass-fibre moon is 59 ft in diameter, and the twenty capsules hold three 'spacemen' each.

94 (previous page) The Big Ferris Wheel. Height 145 ft, diameter 132 ft, operating space 82 ft by 80 ft. It weighs 154,520 tons. This must be one of the largest portable rides made, with its thirty-six cars each holding six adults. When operational the Wheel is mounted on four 40ft containers, and in spite of its size needs no other foundations. In transit these same containers, plus three others, transport the components of the Wheel, exemplifying the brilliant engineering of the Schwarzkopf company.

95 The Big Eli Scrambler. Diameter 60 ft. The twelve aluminium seats each hold two adults. The centre pole of the ride revolves in a clockwise direction at 11 r.p.m. The three sets of cars revolve anti-clockwise. The sensation of speed is enhanced by the seats moving in a 'star' pattern.

George Ferris was head of the Phoenix Iron Works, Pittsburgh, which produced many 150ft 'perpendicular roundabouts'. Wheels of this kind were driven by water power, had observation towers, and even sliding seats.

For the Chicago Exhibition of 1893 Ferris built an enormous Wheel, ostensibly as an engineering feat to rival the Eiffel Tower in Paris. Constructed on an ingenious suspension system, the Wheel was 250ft in diameter, 204ft high, 45ft long, and weighed 140,000 lb. There were 36 cars measuring 36ft by 13ft, each holding 60 people, and the total weight of the Wheel was some 1250 tons!

Power was supplied by a 1000 h.p. steam engine, with another one held in readiness in case of emergency. The speed of the Wheel was an incredible one revolution every 20 minutes, and two complete turns constituted a ride.

The Eli Bridge Company, Jacksonville, Illinois, one of the oldest manufacturers of fairground machines in America, which exports on a world-wide basis, was founded by W. E. Sullivan (1861–1932). He was much impressed by Ferris's Giant Wheel, and the Wheel has always been the firm's main product.

96 Loop-o-Plane. Minimum ground operation area 15 ft 6 in. by 30 ft 6 in.; minimum fence area 19 ft 6 in. by 28 in. Weight approx. 13,800 lb on fifth wheel, 5,800 lb on ride axle.

The main column and base are built up of heavy tubular steel members. The pendulums and counter-weights are made from high-strength steel box sections, and the supporting braces from tubular steel members and plate. To provide protection against corrosion all parts, including the cars, are completely sand-blasted, removing mill scale before the primer coat is applied.

The drive is supplied during operation by a petrol engine equipped with electric starter, generator and battery. This also powers the hydraulic pump which actuates the large cylinder when setting up or dismantling. Friction clutches are engaged manually by the operator to provide two-way operation, through a reversing gear-box which is driven by a fluid coupling attached to the engine. The complete mechanical drive is time-proven and uses components that are interchangeable with those of other rides made by the Eyerley firm.

97 The Rok-o-Plane. Height 45 ft, operating space 44 ft by 40 ft. Weight 24,000 lb. This a later model of the one owned by John Remblance Snr and more than 140 of them have been made since 1948. (Eyerley)

98 The Spider. Height 19 ft 6 in., operating space 56 ft 5 in. One of the latest 'Octopus'-based machines. Since the original idea was patented in 1936 numerous adaptations have been made and more than 400 rides of this type have been produced. The curved arms on this particular model represent not only a visual approach to design, but also contribute to engineering safety. The 'Monster' is another similar variant of the Octopus with six arms and twenty-four cars.

99 The Portable Rim-drive Paratrooper. Height 40 ft, operating space 55 ft by 60 ft. Weight 27,000 lb. All gears and drive shafts have been eliminated from this ride, which also has reverse rotation. Only the cars need be removed when dismantling, as all other parts fold onto the trailer. (Hrubetz)

100 The Portable Slide. Height 29 ft, length 100 ft, width 8 ft. Weight including trailer 18,000 lb. The three 100ft lanes guide 'passengers' down the slide, which is built onto its own 40ft trailer. (Hrubetz)

The first months of 1899 found Sullivan working on drawings for the construction of a transportable Wheel, which when finalized was 45 ft in diameter, with 12 cars. After five years of experimentation, he succeeded in 1905 in producing one which was light, portable, and secured not with bolts but with socket-and-pin connections.

About 1200 Eli Wheels have been made since 1905, and apart from these, there have been many individual machines, notably the Aeroscope of 1917.

Probably the most famous Giant Wheel, which is still operating, is the *Riesenrad* in the Prater, Vienna. It is known the world over through the film *The Third Man*, in which it featured so prominently.

The 'Scrambler', which was introduced by the Eli Bridge Co. in 1954, was in its early stages virtually useless as far as travelling fairs were concerned since the central gearing had to be buried beneath ground level. Re-designing has made the present-day model much simpler to erect.

Perhaps the most significant ride made by Eli is the HT5 Wheel, the whole of which is mounted on a trailer and can be erected by two men using the hydraulic system. When on the road the wheel folds down and is only $12\frac{1}{4}$ feet at its highest point. Levelling the base is made easy by the use of hydraulic jacks. The arms are hinged together; the lamps, electric cable and four of the seats are permanently attached to the machine.

101 The Tip-Top. Height 32 ft, operating space 55 ft square. Weight 37,000 lb. A fast and colourful ride, which consists of a turntable 35 ft in diameter mounted on a hinged frame with huge air cylinders. The ten cars can be spun on their spindles by the passengers themselves. The turntable is rotated at 9 r.p.m., and then thrust from a horizontal position to an angle of 20 degrees by an air cylinder. At this point the air is exhausted to the atmosphere and the ride is allowed to fall on an air cushion which causes it to bounce, much like a rubber ball.

Lee Eyerley, the founder of the Eyerley Aircraft Co., of Salem, Oregon, built several aircraft during the 1920s, ran charter flights and gave flight instruction. He also gave displays of flying at air shows and other celebrations in the general area. In 1929 he invented a ground-based primary flight trainer which he called the Acroplane. Then came the Depression and the demand for flying training on the part of the public fell away. However, it was soon recognized that the machine could be adapted as an amusement device, and fifty-four were made in the following three or four years.

From these beginnings came the Octopus and many other rides, all of which are designed to incorporate or simulate some aerial manoeuvre or sensation of flight. The proprietor of Frank Hrubetz & Co. Inc. of Salem, Oregon was formerly with the Eyerley Aircraft Co. The company was established in 1929 and are the makers of some very impressive rides. They can claim to have been the first to introduce the inclined Wheel, to use an hydraulic system in their rides, and to mount an entire large machine on a trailer.

The Chance Manufacturing Co. Inc. of Wichita, Kansas came onto the scene in 1960, with their miniature steam trains. In 1962 they built the Trabant, the first of the 'thrill' rides, and have since followed this up with many others.

5 THE THEATRE OF MACHINES

What is called playful by those favourably inclined and is condemned as child's play by the serious . . . actually has profound significance. By detaching things from their familiar context, by considering them from hitherto unknown points of view, by employing them without obvious purpose but out of sheer joy in totally different combinations, a resilient creative power is kept alive. And this is what mankind needs when the freezing point has been reached in a tradition which finds itself no longer capable of meeting a newly emergent problem.

Ulrich Conrads and Hans Sperlich,
Fantastic Architecture

102 Air view of 'Welfare State' (see p. 109)

The fairground is a combination of engineering and fantasy; of hard work, business and magic. The devices used, including the machines, 'joints' and 'swag', raise some interesting questions about the nature of industrial archaeology, architecture and technology. A mechanical ride is something which does not fall readily into any one category: art, construction, transport, all three enter into the equation and the answer is not to be found in a single cut-and-dried definition. In these concluding pages I shall briefly consider this aspect of the subject, and explore some of the implications.

As we have seen, a variety of factors contributed to the application of machinery to the fairground. In Great Britain particularly the idea of a machine which was designed and built solely to give pleasure was unusual and something of an anomaly, a by-product of the industrial revolution. The European countries had a history of toy-making to which they could refer, and some of the early mechanical rides seem to have originated in France. The ride is after all only a giant toy, made to create a kind of waking dream, in which everything is out of scale; even the wagons themselves, lined entirely in mahogany, seem like giant furniture from *Alice in Wonderland.*

Historians of fairs are few, and they have all begun by regretting the neglect of the subject by the majority of scholars. There are no books which deal with the fair as myth, sculpture, or, with few exceptions, as serious architecture, and the references to it as popular culture are for the most part only fleeting. By 1885 William Morris, to whom much of technology was anathema, was deeply concerned by the lack of a truly popular art, and yet in the same year many interesting rides were produced. In short, fairs have been excluded from the main literary and theoretical history of art and technology. This was partly owing to scarcity of information, partly because the fair has usually been regarded as a sort of playful nonsense which lay somewhere outside the traditional theatre and was in some way unworthy of study. Henry Morley suggests as much in his introduction to *Bartholomew Fair* (see pp. 12–13). Nevertheless the fame of Frederick Savage, who sent rides as far as Cape Town and engines to Russia, rested securely upon such qualities as adaptability, inventiveness and craftsmanship, not to mention entrepreneurial skill.

This relative silence on the part of historians has left fairground machinery as something of an enigma. The shapes and structures of the machines have always been designed in unique and distinctive styles, free of any formal aesthetic code. They have developed into unusual and sensational parodies of movements and forces, generated with essentially humorous and playful intentions by a vivid and adventurous attitude towards technology. The imagination which conceived of a cage which swished high into the air, driven by powerful steam engines, or designed cars to whirl people into space, or canvas tubes to cover them, had invented technological witticisms. Many of the movements and objects experienced in everyday life have been exaggerated or expressed at some time in a fairground machine. The dance has been the inspiration for the Waltzer and the Brooklyn Cakewalk; boats appear in the Sea-on-Land, and cars on the Switchbacks and Dodgems. The sensations of walking, turning, falling, and floating have prompted the invention of many a ride, yet all of these sensations were transformed in the process of expressing them in mechanical terms.

A machine on a fair is often an evocation of a real phenomenon, but is never a direct imitation and has distortions and characteristics not found in the 'real' world outside. A transformation of this kind can be seen in the early representation of animals. The Anderson horses (see Ill. 7) have enormous vitality and vigour, and yet they are not 'realistically' carved. The ostriches and cockerels which sometimes were substituted for horses are hugely out of scale; they embody various anatomical distortions and are painted in colours which are much brighter than reality would demand. On the horses of J. Noyce's set of Gallopers grotesque and heraldic masks are carved, and during the Boer War many of the equine mounts had their heads replaced by the carved portraits of famous generals. The 'life' with which the equipment is imbued depends upon this transformation of realities into imaginative contexts, where the machine if necessary can become animal in form.

The preceding chapters have shown how the Waltzer developed from the simple revolving discs into the quite extraordinary machines of today. The patents reveal the strange process by which an idea derived from a dance evolved through several mechanical forms, until the final result expressed movement which had no previous equivalent. Even Eyerley's Roll-o-Plane has an effect quite unlike the pilot trainer from which it stemmed (see p. 93). The Big Wheel, which we now take so much for granted, is a remarkable invention which is staggeringly different from the *katcheli* (see p. 16) or water wheels, and the original conception and development of it was the work of imaginative genius. However the sensation experienced on the 'Ferris Wheel' is not exactly that of flying, in that the car, and hence the rider himself, is an integral part of the earthbound machinery.

Among the rides that simulate flight some, like the Eyerley machines, relate directly to aerial manoeuvres; others are simply toys of the imagination such as the Moon Rocket, where no attempt is made to produce the actual physical sensations we associate with a trip to the moon. The cars are shaped like the jets in comics or science fiction books, and the ride is an adaptation of the Ark, tilted at an angle with rockets instead of animals.

The Apollo 14 ride made by Anton Schwarzkopf lies somewhere between the Eyerley planes and the Moon Rockets. Movement is used to simulate a journey, but is not itself the subject of the ride, and the glass-fibre moon is just as important a prop in the general effect. The 'jets', complete with hydraulic hiss are yet another variation on the theme. The decorative jet at the summit of Shaw's 'Jet Star' is ferocious and straight out of 'Dan Dare', and

103 Shaw's Jet Star

104 Shaw's Jet Star, showing structure

the lights which surround its perimeter and the arms of the machine are part of the show. By day the structure of the ride is visible, and the sight of the gears and engineering keeps the rockets 'ground based' in the imagination. By night, however, the mechanical parts disappear into the dark; only the lights are visible as they trace their exotic patterns across the blackness, and the 'jets' themselves become more credible and thrilling.

The whole subject of flight has been the touchstone of inspiration for the ride since the early 'Chairoplanes' with their birds and elaborate 19th-century carriages. At the other end of the scale there were fixed 'Sea-on-Land' machines made with permanent foundations and mechanical drive beneath the water. We have already seen how the rocking and pitching movements of the boat were initiated on the portable ride, but even the boat became airborne in the Steam Swings, known as 'Flying Yachts', which take off in most exuberant style in a sort of mechanical storm.

The motor-car made its first appearance on the Switchback as a replacement for the Gondola in 1905, but the 1920s had found a more expressive form in the Dodgem. Even here, though, the story has a few twists, such as animal-shaped cars and the use of speaking tubes to simulate a movement originally suggested by the petrol engine. Eventually the Dodgem, with its 'promiscuous' movement arrived as the accepted fun-fair image of the motor-vehicle.

The simple bicycle became a Velocipede, which whether steam- or muscle-powered evolved into a curiosity of many guises.

The Velocipede was perhaps the most deceptively simple of ideas, and on the face of it the most innocuous. The basic and most common version comprised a circular row of bicycles which everybody pedalled in order to make it go round. Obviously the more people were on the machine, the faster it revolved. If, however, the lure of the Velocipede was such that you had to indulge your passion with no one to accompany you and share the pedalling, you would have had the greatest difficulty in proceeding at all, let alone with any velocity. Most of these machines were fitted with brakes, operated by the showman, and it is said that one pleasant and peaceful sunny day in the 1890s, when the ride was filled with powerfully built, athletic cyclists pedalling for all they were worth, the brakes failed. Alas, the showman's cries were unheard or unheeded as he exhorted his customers to cease pedalling, with the result that scenes of some violence took place as the former, becoming more and more distraught, tried to grapple with rider after rider as they sped by. This, it is said, only increased their merriment, since they had little difficulty in eluding his grasp as they swept past, only to reappear behind the furious show-

105 Steam Swings at Hull fair

106 The Caterpillar

man once again with taunts and wisecracks which they had plenty of time to think up on the way round. It is to be supposed that in the end the cyclists had to give up out of sheer exhaustion, allowing the showman to have his say at last. His comments are, however, not recorded.

The 'Caterpillars' are the successors to the dragons and peacocks which filled the Scenics, but unlike these monsters the Caterpillar acquired its name because of a coincidental resemblance of the canvas-covered machine to the insect. The speed, the feeling of enclosure, which resembles that experienced in a railway tunnel, are transformed into a game, where the fears of the unknown and the dark are resolved by humour and the occasional gust of wind.

The fair has thus become a theatre of machines, in which mechanical toys are the vehicles for mystery, excitement and thrills. In general the development of the fairground has been one of the few unrestricted areas of human imaginative endeavour, and there are no definitive rules for decoration. When the art and design theorists of the 19th century in England were struggling with the problems of 'correct' ornamentation, the showmen were cheerfully and optimistically painting and carving anything which seemed visually exciting, and they have continued to do so. Yet the results aren't chaotic, but remain rare and beautiful examples of baroque forms in a highly industrialized civilization. The painting of mock architecture with evocations of space has a tradition which goes back to the Italianate work of the 17th century, and may possibly have been brought into England directly by the European sculptors who worked on the decoration of the first Scenics; some of the images have obvious reference to Renaissance and Mannerist painters. The whales (Ill. 52) on the other hand seem to derive from a different source, recalling as they do J. W. M. Turner's sea monsters.

There is nothing to compare with the exhilarating and forceful decoration of the past 30 years, to which a modern ride owes much of its dynamic effect. The painting is now flatter, and derives from a variety of sources. The three-dimensional presence and power of a ride is much more a result of the machine as a whole than of its separate parts, as might have been the case when carved figures were a predominant feature of decoration. The baroque shapes and vivid colours are intensely suggestive of speed and latent energy, and the circular perimeter of a Waltzer encloses a space which is, with lights, music, revolving cars and their occupants, a true sculptural phenomenon. The photographs on this and the succeeding pages show that decoration is multifarious and virtually defies classification. The motor cycles in 'Atha's Modern Speedway' somehow typify the concept 'motor-bike' without being complex or over-

107 Atha's Modern Speedway. Eddy's Speedway is just visible to the right (see Ill. 109 for close-up of its decoration)

108 An Orton-built Speedway

accurate in detail. The wheels are painted as though they were revolving, and the chrome adds to the illusion; the colourful and controlled drawing on the pillars of the ride is representative of painting of a totally different kind which it would be hard to analyze. Obviously the cinema and the ethos of the Giant Screen have had a considerable influence on the shapes and sizes of these elements, but then so have Art Nouveau, heraldic shields and many other usually dissimilar areas of aesthetics.

Neither the decoration nor the architecture has ever been 'monumental' in conception, nor was it made with a view to being preserved for posterity. Indeed ideas and shapes which originally had a 'serious' function have been quietly stolen and made into amusing allusions. The wide pillars on Eddy's Ark are not load-bearing to the extent to which the width might suggest, and the imposing front is a joyful pastiche of cinema, town hall and all the pomp of façade. The pictures of Arthur on John Thurston's early Noah's Ark, the profusion of flags, and the giant Ben Hur, are after all for amusement only.

To the right of the Speedway in Ill. 107 can be seen the edge of an Orton-built machine, with its much less sophisticated painting of landscape and motor-bike. Here the gentleman astride the cycle looks remarkably like Punch, and the clouds of dust apparently billowing from the rear are evocative of a kind of comic haste, as the vehicle

109 Decorations on Eddy's Speedway

plunges on its never-ending journey. This elaborate uniting of colour and form is essential to a fair, where the very qualities of contrast and the collision of disparate elements, which would be disastrous in most situations, are the essence of its vitality. Each step on a fairground brings new surprises, and views which are sometimes stunningly beautiful; no space is unfilled and shapes tower and curve, unfolding with truly amazing versatility. In no other 20th-century western architecture does one find the extraordinary range of forms or the marvellous variety and sharpness of colour, blue, red, yellow, gold and silver.

The patterns seen in Ills. 108–14 make up a curious collection of visual art to be found together at the same time. They were all part of the fair on Woodhouse Moor in Leeds in September 1973. The dragons still made an appearance, but this time reduced from their terrifying size, and placed alongside the toy bikes. The two-dimensional surfaces are filled with shapes which seem always to burst into three dimensions, using all possible trickery and an optical illusion. The electrifying forms on the paybox of Shaw's Dodgems appear to twist and explode into space with hypnotic abundance, and the stars and stripes on the Moon Rocket accentuate the already enormous height of the back surface. The colours and drawings are the devices by which 'magic' is transmitted to a machine, giving it life and creating illusion on all its surfaces.

110 Decorations on Eddy's converted Speedway, showing the cars as designed and painted by the owners

111 Cars from a Maxwell-built Waltzer

112 Atha's and Eddy's Speedways

VALVOLINE
EDDY'S

113 Close-up of the rear of the paybox for Shaw's Dodgems

114 Shaw's Moonrocket. The cars, which pivot and swing outward under centrifugal force, were designed by the owners.

As was shown in the previous chapter the American rides are often bare in comparison with their British equivalents. The 'Meteorite' was manufactured in the U.S.A. and was completely devoid of decoration when it was imported into England. Now it has a platform built round it, which both allows passengers ease of access, and provides a screen for embellishment. When I saw the ride at Leeds, the owner was busily painting stars on to the underneath so that they would be visible when the ride was raised above the ground.

Although it is possible to manufacture machines without any but the most simple decoration, they would not be in the real fairground tradition, which has its roots firmly in visual entertainment. The exciting image has always been an indivisible part of the fair as a whole, and the answers to questions about the purpose of a ride are to be found as much in the colourful shapes as in the mechanical parts. The decorative rocket on the top of Shaw's Jets is in this sense functional, since it contributes to the over-all dynamic objective, and the machine has therefore extended into painting and sculpture.

At a very simple level the fair must contain the dreams and true mythological character of the age to which it

115 The Meteorite

belongs; otherwise no one would be attracted and the fair would close. Everything, from the smallest toy to be won on the darts, to the largest of the machines is a part of the same structured fantasy world, which is full of miniature aeroplanes, huge caterpillars and space-bound rockets. The current and popular discotheque Waltzers are merely the next in a succession of machines which have had a direct relationship with the popular imagination, and music has been an essential part of the atmosphere ever since the travelling musicians with Sedgwick's menagerie contributed to the show and spectacle, and indeed long before that. In 1898 the paper-operated organs made by Marenghi or Gavioli superseded the trumpet organ on the front of the great Bioscope shows. By the 1920s they were playing songs like 'You made me love you' on the Scenics. The Swings of 1904 had Aeolian harps on the cars which would be played by the wind as the speed of the ride increased, and the modern siren is a more aggressive version of the same idea. Recorded music is compact and effective, and as the new rides are a product of urban rather than agricultural societies, it is appropriate that the music should be Pop, Rock, and Soul, which grew up in the same environment.

The new rides do not necessarily replace the older ones; new and old stand cheek by jowl without creating any feelings of discord. Thus the Jets find themselves in close proximity to the Gallopers, and the 'Flying Yachts' – still a very exciting ride – are not far away. As in a dream the definitions usually imposed by time and history do not seem to apply during the few hours when a fair is open. The sensations and experiences to be found there, which thrust themselves upon all the senses, are created by the oddities of scale, the colours, the alternate light and darkness, and the music; but principally by movement, which is ultimately the common factor among all fairs in all ages.

It is clear that two basic considerations alone should determine how the pleasure machine develops. It must fulfil its appropriate mythological or allegorical role and be attractive to its generation; but at the same time it must be practical, simple in construction and allow numbers of people to ride together safely. The various adaptations (Ills. 55–60) are responses to these essential requirements, and the rides described and illustrated in chapter 3 were, many of them, unsuited for use on a travelling fair because they failed in some way to meet these requirements. Most of the changes have taken place as a result of the insight of the showmen who were close enough to the rides to see and understand the realities of the business and convey these to the most sympathetic or receptive manufacturers. The resulting equipment is a unique combination of compact precision and mysterious flamboyance, which endows the fair with the ability to change and expand continuously beyond itself. It has often been a focus for more wide-ranging activities, and a full-size hot-air balloon which left Docking Fair in the summer of 1972 was only one example of the extended entertainment the non-finite character of the fair offers. A 30ft showman's wagon, originally built by Paisley & Shilling in Dumfries, Scotland in about 1962, recently found itself in a more unorthodox situation when it was bought by John Fox, who is the director of a performing arts group called 'Welfare State'. The wagon, complete with mahogany and cut glass windows, has proved to be the only type of mobile home which can sustain the tremendously lengthy journeys of this avant-garde theatre, as it travels widely in Great Britain and into Europe.

'Welfare State' (Ill. 102) is run by artists who specialize in recreating myths, using pantomime, street theatre and multi-media compositions. In part this sort of activity is a rebirth of the older kind of fair where fire-eaters, entertainers and dancers predominated. The scenes created are a hybrid mixture of circus and surrealist spectacle, and the poster announcing the opening of the 'Travels of Lancelot Quail' owes as much to the pre-industrial fairground as it does to the rarefied atmosphere of 20th-century art. The equipment which the group uses, including wagons, caravans, lorries, generators and the circus tent, provides a physical and conceptual framework around which the experimental inventions can develop. Since 1968 when 'Welfare State' was formed, they have had success with many events, from 'The Marriage of Heaven and Hell', to several 'Naming Ceremonies'; many versions of 'Earth-rise' and the more recent 'Lancelot Quail' adventure.

On September 1st 1972 they set off on a month-long trek across the West Country, following the route from Glastonbury to St Michael's Mount which was reputedly taken by Phoenician tin traders, and has links with the legends of King Arthur and Joseph of Arimathea. The line is also allegedly one of the ley lines which Alfred Watkins has described, and which were invested with magical significance in the pre-Christian religions of the Britons. The journey itself was conceived of as one continuous performance presenting in natural surroundings events and images from the life of the 'backstreet hero' Quail. Rituals were enacted at prehistoric monuments or sites, and performances were held in the main circus tent describing in microcosm the whole journey in which appeared characters such as Death, the Devil, Merlin the Keeper of Time, sundry dragons, 'freaks', scarecrows and 'technological giants'. A submarine, which may seem a little out of context, was loaned by the Navy, and became the stage upon which the Fool and the Hero followed their inevitable destinies.

The myths and stories with which 'Welfare State' make their 'civic magic' are partly invented and partly inherited. The obvious tradition of mummer's plays and travelling theatre has been fragmented by the 'technological giants' of the industrial revolution. Vestiges remain only in some folk songs, in local legends and festivals. It is ironic but appropriate that the spirit of the older forms of the theatre should be carried into the 20th century by the machines of the fairs, and that this equipment should be capable of transmitting powerful artistic statements to the modern world.

The term 'popular art' is often used to describe art which is in some way of a lesser order. Perhaps the photographs, information and ideas collected here will give an opportunity for the fairground machine to be re-appraised as painting, sculpture and architecture, which at its best is as exciting as any seen in public galleries or in the towns and cities. We have seen that the fair is a mobile town which exists in infinitely variable size, time and space. There is another aspect which is often overlooked. Most of the few extant mobile generators of electricity belong to showmen, and at critical times many industries, including the Post Office, have had recourse to them when mains supplies have failed. In recent emergencies it has been brought home to the public how dependent society is upon the normal supply systems, which allow little room for adaptation in a crisis, and the fact that the present owners of showmen's steam engines fitted with generators can produce electricity and remain unaffected by power cuts or oil shortages should not be disregarded.

The acceptance of the wagon and fairground machine as architecture requires an imaginative step which, once taken, releases ideas that have remained for the most part dormant within the mainstream of the history of building, and allows a much broader concept of architecture to emerge; one which includes many things from rococo fantasy to the pure machine. The possibility of having industrially produced mobile houses has existed as an idea in architectural theory for a very long time, at least since Paxton's Crystal Palace, but has scarcely been examined and accepted as a serious proposition on a domestic level except by the showmen. The homes in which most of us live are built in cubical forms from bricks, and take a relatively long time to construct. In a period when land, materials and time are at a premium it would be an advantage to adopt a more imaginative approach to the forms and methods used for making our shelter, and build houses or parts of houses which can respond to need and circumstance, changing or moving in relationship with the existing traditional and static structures. An analysis of the housing situation might show that the shortage and lack of variety is caused partly by the severe constraints under which imagination in architecture has been operating for so long. The psychological barriers to mobile or prefabricated architecture might disappear with the realization that it is human in quality, and has been with us for over a century disguised as places of amusement, in a multitude of forms and colours wildly different from the box shapes which dominate most of our living spaces. The familiar dream in which we run away to join the fair is partly an expression of the desire to live in a mobile society, and the fairground architecture that expresses the nomadic and fantastic instincts is a language which we could all learn if we chose to do so. The fairs have an architectural importance as a continuous and highly successful experiment, and offer a point of departure for a serious study of buildings as far apart as those of Ferdinand Cheval and Buckminster Fuller. As an example of parallel and neglected constructional developments it is instructive to compare the photographs of some of the rides – for example the Swirl in process of erection (Ill. 116) – with Buckminster Fuller's Dymaxion house of 1944 (Ill. 117).

There have been many experiments along these lines since 1944, but in few fields have they been so consistently carried out as in the manufacture of amusement equipment or actually on a travelling fair, where necessity has produced the impetus and where prefabrication does not mean greyness or ultimate uniformity. The vivid and consciously egotistical letters standing out against the sky on Eddy's Speedway (Ill. 110) are a long way from the world of modern experimental architecture, and they are much more indivi-

116 The Swirl being erected at Long Melford, Suffolk

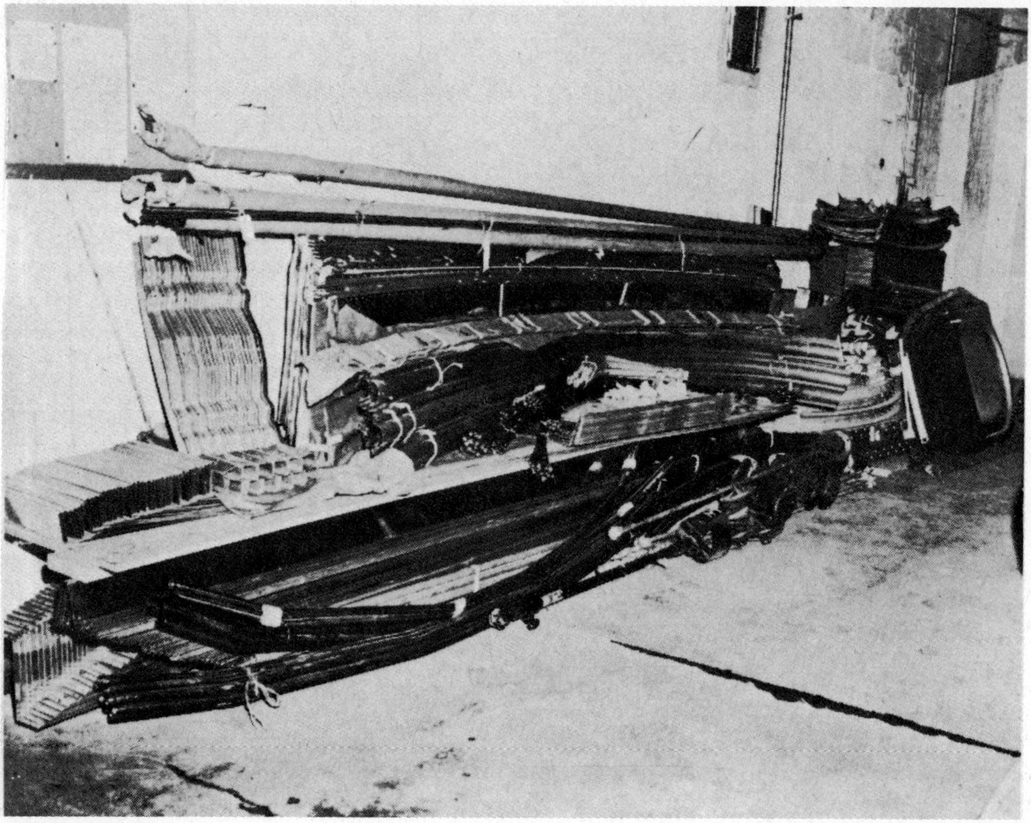

117 Buckminster Fuller's Dymaxion House in course of erection *c.* 1944

dual and resilient. Indeed this is the crux of the matter; the kind of statement that Fuller was making in the 1930s and 1940s, which so startled the architectural world, might have been well comprehended by showmen of 1890. The showman's discovery of nomadic and prefabricated forms pre-dates Fuller's discovery of kinetic architecture by some fifty years.

If there is a final paradox of which the fairs are an expression it is that the temporary and mobile structures of the fairground have proved in some ways to have greater continuity and potential or actual permanence than the towns and cities through which they move. Were it possible to make a film of the centre of almost any city in Great Britain covering the last two to ten decades and if this film were to be replayed at a vastly increased speed, it would show that, while fixed buildings have much in common with the fair, there is one vital difference: once pulled down they rarely go up again. Fairground machines show that prefabricated architecture need not be disposable or 'throw-away', and a ride such as the Gallopers would make repeated appearances throughout the hypothetical film. In the conventional use of materials in the building of vehicles and houses the waste of energy since the Industrial Revolution

118 Bennett's Mapperley factory. The jigs used for making Ivan Bennett's machines are standardized for complete accuracy in the construction of the various sections of a ride. When slotted together the sections must fit with as much strength as a welded joint, while at the same time remaining free enough to be easily assembled and dismantled. This is a clear demonstration of the principle of continuous tension which is so important in kinetic architecture. The factory itself shows how simple the basic equipment need be for the production of large spatial structures. 'System' is the key to an understanding of this process, and of the mobile fairground.

has been enormous and tragic. The suggestion implicit in the preceding speculation is that fairs are a product of change, and that fairground life has produced an architecture of survival. Though mistakes have been made as in other spheres, as far as possible rides have been adapted and parts re-used as an alternative to destruction.

Our imaginary film might show ways in which existing older houses for example could have been adapted in a more pragmatic and creative way by using modern materials instead of being expensively and finally obliterated. There are many ways in which prefabrication of re-usable and mobile parts might be effected; and Fuller's bathroom unit, Armstrong's container unit (p. 18) or Maxwell's Waltzer (Ill. 85), show in their different ways that a more adventurous imagination might result in a more interesting and useful architecture. If it is true, as Lewis Mumford has suggested, that a great many important ideas reveal themselves in play, where alternatives are always more apparent, then it might be useful to approach technology and architecture as though they were the toys and fantasies which they may well be.

In 1874 Thomas Frost wrote that the last showman was in imminent danger of being exhibited himself, as a being so

119 Reflected in the faces of these children on a roundabout is all the magic, joy and wonder of the fair.

unusual as to be worthy of viewing by those in search of the curious. The amusement ride gave the fairs new life, and the last hundred years have seen the flowering of a number of remarkably beautiful machines. The basic technologies may soon change again, but the gaiety and humanity of the fair is endlessly regenerative, and the next hundred years will doubtless see the emergence of even more startling inventions to astonish and delight future generations. The equipment illustrated and described in this book is a tribute to the inventiveness of those who build and operate the travelling fairs; they are the inheritors of the same truly artistic tradition that produced the Bioscope shows or the Scenics.

The fairs are genuine festivals which have survived the repressive attention of the authorities for hundreds of years, and if their existence as cultural phenomena has been overlooked by historians, it has never been neglected by children, who have an instinctive grasp of what they are all about.

TOY TOWN TOURS

APPENDIX 1

For detailed information of fairs operating during the season, the best source to consult is the 'Coming Events' page in *The World's Fair* each week, which is available by order from any newsagent. The list that follows, however, though by no means complete, records some of the events which take place, and demonstrates the wide geography of activity which forms the annual and repeated spiral of fairground location. The fairs can vary in size from the small country fair with only two or three machines, to the major events, like those held at Hull, Newcastle and Nottingham, which may have 40 to 50 machines.

February

King's Lynn Mart
Lichfield Fair (Staffs)
Holbeck Fair (Yorks)
Downham Market Fair (Norfolk)
Stalybridge Fair (Cheshire)
Orrell Fair, Wigan (Lancs)
Langton Shrovetide Fair (Staffs)

March

Lichfield Shrovetide Fair
Wisbech Mart
Holbeck (Yorks)
Stockport Fair (Lancs)
Clay Cross (Derbyshire)
Pontadawe Fair (Glamorgan)
Crawley Fair (Sussex)
Haddington Fair (E. Lothian)
Dumfries March Fair
Stainforth Market Fair (Yorks)
Victoria Park Fair (London)
Whittlesey Spring Fair, Isle of Ely
Doncaster (Racecourse) Gala Day Fair (Yorks)
Chipping Sodbury Fair (Glos)

April

Stamford-mid-Lent Fair
Worksop Fair (Notts)
Falkirk Fair (Stirling)
Bo'ness Spring Fair (Midlothian)
Colne Fair (Lancs)
Devizes Fair (Wilts)
Grantham-mid-Lent Fair
Clapham Common Fair (London)
Andover Fair (Hants)
Scunthorpe Fair (Lincs)
(Easter Fairs)
Plymouth (Devon)
Kirkaldy Links Market (Fife)
Norwich (Norfolk)
Cambridge
Lincoln
Mottingham (London)
Lea Bridge (London)
Hampstead Heath (London)
Woodhouse (Leeds)
Heath Common (Yorks)
Newcastle upon Tyne

May

Lowestoft (Suffolk)
Rugby (Warwicks)
Bristol (Oldbury Court) (Somerset)
Neilston Fair (Renfrew)
Atherton Fair (Lancs)
Oakham Fair (Rutland)
Putney Fair (London)
Wells Fair (Somerset)
Hereford Fair
Stow-on-the-Wold Fair (Glos)
Glasgow
Abergavenny Fair
Brighton Fair (Sussex)
Midsomer Norton Fair (Somerset)
Crystal Palace May Fair (London)

June

Bristol Midsummer Fair
Epsom Fair (Surrey)
Wimbledon Fair (London)
Stanwell Donkey Derby and Fair (Middlesex)
Welsh Old Time Festival and Steam Fair (Cardiff)
Doncaster Fair (Yorks)
Cornwall Royal Show (Wadebridge)

Towcester Fair (Northampton)
Peterborough Cherry Fair
Windsor Carnival and Fair (Berks)
Ashford Fair (Kent)
Usk Trinity Fair (Monmouth)
Streatham Common Festival Week Fair (London)
Lakenheath Carnival and Fair (Suffolk)

July

Wimborne Carnival and Fair (Dorset)
Henley Regatta and Fair (Oxon)
Dartmouth Carnival and Fair (Devon)
Cheltenham Festival and Fair (Glos)
Chapeltown Fair (Yorks)
Poole Regatta and Fair (Dorset)
Stratford-upon-Avon Edwardian Steam Fair (Warwicks)
Billericay Carnival and Fair (Essex)
Praze Fair (Cornwall)
Glossop Summer Event (Derbyshire)
Haywards Heath Carnival and Fair (Sussex)
Chester-le-Street Fair (Co. Durham)
Buckley Jubilee Club Fair (Flint)
Spennymoor Gala and Fair (Co. Durham)

August

Sleaford Fair (Lincs)
Bournemouth Regatta Carnival and Fair (Hants)
Wakefield Fair (Yorks)
Christchurch Fair (Hants)
Babbacombe Regatta and Fair (Devon)
Consett Show and Fair (Co. Durham)
Southend-on-Sea Carnival and Fair (Essex)
Crieff Games Fair (Perth)
Mostyn Carnival and Fair (Flint)
Rothesay High Games (Clyde)
St Andrew Lammas Fair (Fife)
Sturminster Newton Carnival and Fair (Dorset)
Rochdale Festival (Lancs)
Haywards Heath Fair (Sussex)
Mitcham Common Fair (London)

September

Helston Harvest Fair (Cornwall)
Barnet Fair (Herts)
Greenwich Show, Carnival and Fair (London)
Pengover Rally (Cornwall)
Cheddar Fair (Somerset)
Doncaster St Leger Fair (Yorks)
Truro Festival week (Cornwall)
Widecombe Fair (Devon)
Laibert Tryst Fair (Stirling)
Glastonbury Tor Fair (Somerset)
Matlock Fair (Derbyshire)
Kirkcudbright Fair
Newton Abbott Cheese and Onion Fair (Devon)
Annesley Miners' Gala and Fair (Notts)
Barnstaple Fair (Devon)

October

Poole Fair (Dorset)
Menai Bridge Fair (Anglesey)
Gainsborough Fair (Lincs)
Crawley Fair (Sussex)
Peterborough Bridge Fair (Northants)
Stratford-upon-Avon Mop Fair (Warwicks)
Ely Fair (Cambs)
Llanlcechid Fair (Caernarvon)
Daventry Mop Fair (Northants)
Sherborne Pack Fair (Dorset)
St Albans Steam Engine Rally (Herts)
Abingdon Michaelmas Fair (Berks)
Cirencester 1st Mop Fair (Glos)
Marlborough Little Mop Fair (Wilts)
Pudsey (Bonfire) Fair (Yorks)

November

Birmingham (Sunnyfield Park) Fair
Hythe Fair (Kent)
Belper Fair (Derbyshire)
Aylesbury Fair (Bucks)
Kirton Bonfire and Fair (Notts)

December

Kennington Oval Fair (London)
Kelvin Hall Carnival and Circus (Glasgow)
Northampton Christmas and New Year Fair
Sheffield (Bridgehouses Car Park) Fair
Norwich Xmas Fair
Leicester (Granby Hall) Circus and Fair
Wrexham Xmas Fair (Denbigh)
Wolverhampton Xmas and New Year Fair (Staffs)

APPENDIX 2

King's Lynn Mart

The fair may be well over a thousand years old; King's Lynn, originally known as Saxon Lynn, was well placed for trade with European cities, and also for the inland routes to the Midlands in England. The market was one of the greatest in Europe; as well known and regarded as the ones at Leipzig or Nizhni Novgorod. A charter was granted by King John and another by Henry VIII in 1537. Since the 18th century the date of commencement has been altered from the February 2 to 14. During the late 19th and early 20th centuries the fair saw the debut of many machines made by Savage & Co., including the Gallopers now owned by J. Noyce (pp. 40–2), the electric scenics of E. Farrer, Jacob Studt, W. Murphy, G. T. Tuby, Relph & Pedley, and Fred Gray's Motor Car Scenic in 1920. (This ride was still in use in 1954.)

Between 1920 and the early 1930s, years that were crucial in the development of the fairground ride, many changes took place at King's Lynn Mart. Listed below are some of the new machines, and the year in which they came into use.

1920

Fred Gray's Scenic and Cakewalk
Charles Thurston's Golden Dragons
R. Sedgwick's Slip
G. T. Tuby's Horses
Thurston & Abbott's Gondolas, with traction centre 'Empress' (see p. 120)
Barker & Thurston's Steam Motors
H. Richard's Cakewalk
C. Part's Horses
V. W. Waddington's Yachts

1921

Turner's Razzle Dazzle
C. Abbott's Cakewalk
F. Thompson's Cakewalk
Abbott's Spinning Top Gondolas; this time converted to an electric Scenic
(The traction centre 'Empress' worked as an ordinary show engine with Burrell No. 3285 (King George V))
Richard's Cakewalk
Sedgwick's Slip

1922

J. King's Yachts (brand new)
Barker and Farrar's Chairoplane. (The first to appear in this country)
J. Farrar's Gallopers
H. Richard's Razzle Dazzle and Cakewalk

1923

Charles Thurston's Dragons
Stocks's Gallopers
C. Abbott's Electric Gondolas and Cakewalk
Sedgwick's Slip
Barker & Farrer's Chairs
Farrer's Dragon Scenic and Gallopers
Waddington's Yachts
Thompson's Cakewalk

1924

C. Thurston's Scenic had the dragon cars replaced by peacocks. E. Farrer had a new Whale Scenic and there was a Caterpillar owned by P. Collins

1925

The first petrol lorries came with Richard's Cakewalk and Wolff's Over-the-Falls

1927

Four F. W. D. lorries appeared with Lennard's and C. Thurston's 'Jolly Tubes'

1928
Pat Collins presented a continental type of 'Swish' powered by a large Fowler steam engine

1929
Thurston's Peacocks came for the last time. C. Thurston's and W. Wilson's Dodgems were the first to come to the Mart

1930
Enoch Farrer brought the 'Whales' which, as history would have it, were the last of the Scenics to visit King's Lynn. Farrer also brought a Swirl. Other rides were W. Wilson's Dodgems, Dosnos' Hall of Death and The Globe of Death of P. Collins

1931
Farrer brought the Ark, Dodgems and Swirl

The steam engine continued in diminishing use; in 1922 there had been 17 engines and five steam wagons; in 1923 28 engines; but by 1939 there were only four, after which none except for exhibition purposes.

APPENDIX 3

The chronological summary that follows gives an interesting picture of the sort of equipment which belonged to one of the well-known fairground families over the period of the greatest change – the first four decades of this century. The rides and the nature of the changes which they underwent are much too complex to describe in detail. The history of even one engine, 'Alexandra', from its original position with the Bioscope show in 1901 to its eventual sale to George Cushing in 1947, is a revelation. Until the late 1930s the steam-powered 'Big' and 'Little Machines' (p. 121) were the main rides travelled by Charles Thurston & Sons, after which the Swirl and Dodgems, etc. took over.

The firm of Charles Thurston & Sons began as a partnership between Charles Thurston and John Barker whose first ride was a steam-driven Gondola Switchback built by Tidman's of Norwich, which became known as the 'Little Machine'. The Tidman central engine proving not strong enough to pull the cars at any speed, it was replaced by a Savage centre engine. Until 1909 this ride was transported from place to place by rail.

1897 Another Gondola Switchback acquired, powered by the Savage traction centre 'Empress'.
1901 The first of Charles Thurston's Bioscope shows was bought; it was a two-wagon show front, with a Gavioli organ, all powered by the steam engine 'Alexandra'.

Other rides during the next few years included a bicycle roundabout, which was powered by two motor cycles within the circle; Flying Pigs and Waltzing Balloons, a Helter Skelter and a Brooklyn Cakewalk; another large steam engine, Edward VII, was also introduced.

1908 This year saw the arrival of the 'Great Show', made by Orton Sons & Spooner: it was fitted with a 120-key Marenghi organ, and with an array of coloured lights which made it technically the forerunner of the Discotheque light show. In company with the show already purchased in 1901, it travelled until 1914.
1910 Another Burrell engine, 'Unity' was added.
1919 A Joywheel and the 'Little Machine' travelled together.
1920 At King's Lynn Mart a new electric-driven Golden Dragon Scenic appeared (the 'Big Machine') built by Orton & Spooner. A new Burrell engine 'Victory' with the dynamo and car lifting gear came with the ride; and the other Burrell 'Edward VII' also helped power the ride.

1922 The Joywheel was abandoned, and the Helter-Skelter was brought out again; a new set of Chairoplanes was acquired to be driven by 'Alexandra'.

1923 The Dragon cars of the 'Big Machine' were damaged by fire on the railway at Bletchley, and were replaced by peacock-shaped cars. The Chairoplanes proved unsuccessful and were sold; 'Alexandra' was used to pull the 'Big Machine', to enable the whole ride to travel by road.

1926 A set of 'Jolly Tubes' was acquired. Basically this ride consisted of two large tubes, placed end-to-end and revolving in different directions, through which people walked. This ride was the first to be transported by an F.W.D. lorry.

By *1928* the main rides were the 'Big Machine', the 'Little Machine' and the 'Jolly Tubes'.

1929 A small Burrell and a Garrett steam engine were disposed of and replaced by an F. W. D. lorry, and a Liberty U.S.A. lorry. The 'Little Machine' was altered, motor cars being replaced with swans, dragons and gondolas. At Cambridge midsummer fair a new eight-car Swirl was delivered, and was powered by the Burrell engine 'Alexandra'. This year was obviously a significant one, with the appearance of the new ride and the diesel lorries.

1930 The 'Big Machine' stayed in and some Orton-built Dodgems visited King's Lynn in their place, with the Burrell 'Edward VII'. Both the 'Big Machine' and the 'Little Machine' appeared at Norwich Easter Fair, but this was the last appearance of the 'Little Machine'.

1931 At Downham Market a new (Lakin-built) set of Dodgems appeared and an Orton-built Noah's Ark with 'Victory'.

1933 The Ark was disposed of, and a Waltzer was purchased to take its place.

1934 The Swirl was sold and 'Alexandra' overhauled.

1935 A new Lakin-built Ark was seen at Kettering Feast driven by 'Alexandra'.

The Orton-built Dodgems were sold and a new set by Langwheels was acquired. In 1937 these were sold also. The engine 'Edward VII' stayed in the yard and two Armstrong Saurer diesel lorries took its place. During World War II some of the rides appeared at 'black-out' fairs, but not until 1946 did business return to normal, by which time both the 'Big Machine' and 'Little Machine' had been sold to Butlins. By July 1946 'Alexandra', the only remaining steam engine, was replaced by the Diamond T (p. 35). In 1947 the eight-car Swirl was delivered (Ill. 72). In December of the same year the three Burrell engines, 'Alexandra', 'Victory' and 'Unity' were sold to George Cushing, in whose ownership they remain.

ACKNOWLEDGMENTS

Older photographs have come from many sources, including the private collections of travelling showmen, or of individual collectors such as Mr J. R. Leeson. Permission was also given for reproduction of photographs of historical interest by the Fairground Society, and the Laing Museum, Newcastle-upon-Tyne. Recent photographs in chapter 2 were taken by the author, and most of those in chapter 5 by Bill Major, Lecturer in Fine Art, Leeds Polytechnic. Grateful thanks are due to Mr David Goodale who went to considerable trouble to obtain the delightful photograph (Ill. 119) with which the book closes. Manufacturers of fairground equipment have all given freely of information and photographs. The Patent Office have also been extremely helpful.

Every attempt has been made to give appropriate acknowledgment to those who have given permission for publication of picture material. It does happen occasionally that copyright is obscure, and apologies are extended to anyone whose name has been unintentionally omitted.

SOURCES

The best sources have been all those involved in the manufacture and use of fairground equipment. It might be useful to add that Hall and Fowle, Showmen's Decorators, whose work figures in many of the newer illustrations, operate from Balham High Street, London.

The World's Fair is a focus of all kinds of information, and publishes many useful addresses of societies and organizations interested in the study of various aspects of fairground life. There are still in existence some magazines of the now non-functioning British Fairground Society, which are important factual records.

At the time of writing the main museum of fairground art is at Wookey Hole, Somerset, and another is in the process of formation at King's Lynn, Norfolk.

The undermentioned publications have proved essential reading, and are only a few from the now rapidly growing list of books and articles about fairs and their history.

P. W. Bradley Some notes on the Development of Fairground Machinery. *The Engineer*, 1954, 1955, 1957.

D. Braithwaite *Fairground Architecture.* Hugh Evelyn, London, 1968.

R. Clark *Savages Ltd 1850–1964.* Modern Press, Norwich, 1965.

T. F. G. Dexter *The Pagan Origins of Fairs.* New Knowledge Press, Perranporth, 1930.

Arthur Fay *Bioscope Shows and their Engines.* Oakwood Press, Lingfield, 1966.

Barbara Jones *The Unsophisticated Arts.* Architectural Press, London 1951.

Henry Morley *Memoirs of Bartholomew Fair.* Chapman and Hall, London 1859.

Thomas Murphy M.B.E. The Evolution of the Amusement Machines. *R. A. Arts Journal*, 7 September 1951.

George Sanger *Seventy Years a Showman.* Dent, London 1926.

Alfred Watkins *The Old Straight Track* (1925), reprinted Garnstone Press, London 1972.

INDEX

Italic numbers refer to illustrations and their captions